"The Divine Father" is a must read for everyone who wants to contribute to a harmonious, non-violent society where loving collaboration prevails. The book will inspire both men and women to let go of fear and embrace the reality that we are one. The daily sutras, prayers, contemplations and invocations are wonderful tools to sustain the true masculine energy in all of us.

Cloe Madanes, author of Relationship Breakthrough.

Divine Father is filled with wisdom, heart, and a world of uplifting ideas. Men will surely benefit from these noble ideas and exercises, and women will gain much too. Thank you, Ivonne, for offering vision, inspiration, practical tools, and hope. Surely the world will be better for readers absorbing and living these noble truths.

Alan Cohen, author of A Deep Breath of Life.

Divine Father and Divine Mother… the proverbial two… that are really one. In truth, both relative polarities are the same consciousness and are eternally unified as one. Human beings, however, experience an illusory separation that results in imbalance, fragmentation, conflict, problems and suffering. Since wholeness is proportional to balance and fulfillment is proportional to wholeness, our mastery of the balance principle is imperative to the evolution of our consciousness. I trust that this wonderful book by Ivonne Delaflor will inspire many to create balance as the basis of true holistic experience and its resultant fulfillment.

Master Charles Cannon, Spiritual Director of Synchronicity Foundation for Modern Spirituality http://www.synchronicity.org

The Divine Father book is filled with powerful energy. It feels like an energetical stream of shaktipat, for there are so many sacred words in each text and such a powerful invocation of all the different aspects of the Male Energy, that it actually feels like it's being Downloaded to ones own field as one reads.

Alex Slucki, Aka Swami Ramananda
Author The Color of Your Soul
www.heavenonearthproject.net

At first glance I wasn't sure about Divine Father. I wasn't sure if it was a book, a workbook, a journal, a process, or some combination of them all. As I read through it, contemplating the important messages contained on its pages, I became sure. I became sure that for me it was all of the above and more.

Divine Father was an opportunity for me to explore masculinity, the male spirit, and the relationship between feminine and masculine energy. It was an opportunity for me to reflect, to examine what I think and believe about what it means to be a man in today's world, how and when I stifle that spirit, and what I can do to touch and release the Divine Father that exists within me. It was an opportunity for me to reflect on the important concepts of balance, my changing role of son, spouse, father, grandfather and all the masculine possibilities that still exist for each of us.

Tender, elder, warrior, protector, strength, peaceful, action, silence, support, uniqueness, gentle, awake, longing, harmonic, presence, and more. So much to contemplate. Such an opportunity. Thank you.

Chick Moorman, Author of Parent Talk, Talk Sense
to yourself and many more www.chickmoorman.com

DIVINE FATHER

Reawakening the Balanced Male Spirit & Sacred Mind of Humanity

By Ivonne Delaflor Alexander

Author of Divine Mother &
The Positive Child; Through The Language of Love

iUniverse, Inc.
Bloomington

DIVINE FATHER
REAWAKENING THE BALANCED MALE SPIRIT & SACRED MIND OF HUMANITY

iUniverse books may be ordered through booksellers or by contacting:

iUniverse
1663 Liberty Drive
Bloomington, IN 47403
www.iuniverse.com
1-800-Authors (1-800-288-4677)

Because of the dynamic nature of the Internet, any web addresses or links contained in this book may have changed since publication and may no longer be valid. The views expressed in this work are solely those of the author and do not necessarily reflect the views of the publisher, and the publisher hereby disclaims any responsibility for them.

Any people depicted in stock imagery provided by Thinkstock are models, and such images are being used for illustrative purposes only.

Certain stock imagery © Thinkstock.

ISBN: 978-1-4759-6162-1 (sc)
ISBN: 978-1-4759-6163-8 (e)

Printed in the United States of America

iUniverse rev. date: 01/22/2013

Dedication

To the Awakened Man; the Non Violent
Warrior; The Spirit of Creation.

Acknowledgments

We thank you Father that you are in us and we are in you;
that through us Your Will is sent forth on wings of power;
that Your Purpose is accomplished on earth as it is in heaven;
that through us Your Light and Love and Power is manifest
to all the Sons and Daughters of Mankind. As there will
be 144,000 and more who will feel the Light and Love and
Power of the Father-Mother God and allow themselves to be
a note played within the music of the spheres. J J Dewey

To my Father Noe, for his presence, love and the gift of life.
To my Husband, and Love of My life, Toby Alexander.

His love increases my respect towards the male energy as I embrace deeper, in the now, the power of being a Woman.

I pay tribute to my daughter Alhia, for the inspiration she is and the opportunity for me to realize on how great it is to write a book dedicated to the male energy thinking of her.

To my son Christian, I see, and recognize the master within you, and I am blessed to witness that my journey as a mother is to love you as my child and to Iam, my son, my eagerness to respect male energy has been rebirthed as you are born in the planet in these auspicious times. Your existence motivates me to serve my family and humanity even more!

To Chick Moorman, for the motivation, modeling, and inspiration his presence gave me to write this book.

To Stefan Hermann, an amazing teacher for me, a man with deep integrity who loves his family, who leads the men towards peace and non violence, a supporter of young boys, sacred rituals and initiation, and a reverent observer of rites of passage for humanity, a true warrior.

To Serena Sutherland for always recognizing and motivating others to realize the importance of the father within the sacred portal called family.

To all the men that have rebirthed in T.R[1]

To all the women who have forgiven men, their fathers...and are willing to embrace their own feminine power to support also the male energy in the world.

To all the fathers who are living life as a role model of respect, grace, courage, honesty, integrity, and elegance.

To those who are single parenting their children.

To Enrique, may you always be happy.

To all T.R Trainers...you are remarkable human beings!

To ALL my teachers.

To Alex Slucki (Aka) Swami Ramananda, Cloe Madanes, Alan Cohen & Dan Brule for their time invested to read the book in its non-edited form and write their testimonials from their hearts. I am extremely grateful for your energy presence within this book.

To Master Charles Cannon, for his impeccable modeling of congruency.

To Ray Castellino, my life truly is better because of your teachings and guidance.

To all of the extraordinary people that shared their own heart felt words dedicated to their fathers and that are shared here in this book; Thank you all!

And to all men who have no excuses, the initiated warriors in to non-violence, those who are filled with determination and truth and are here to walk the path of modeling of respect, of humility in the journey of life. As a female embodiment of source and women representative, I thank you deeply for the safety you bring us all and for the important part and role you play for our human family and the ascension of human consciousness.

---

1   T.R; Transcendental Rebirthing System Is a sacred, safe, and supported environment where any human being, no matter the experience he/she has had, is able to explore their birth and beyond with the support of a conscious team which in this method we call sacred womb-mates. The transmutation of Ids, created by the beliefs of traumatic experiences, analogical states of mind, disintegrations, or subconscious assumptions in T.R are immediately transmuted and elevated in to golden nuggets of wisdom, leading towards integration, realization and absolute recognition of that which truly belongs to an individual to work on in divine timing and absolute mature adult-ship. The inner child is acknowledged all the way through this process, in which the person in turn to rebirth is supported whole-heartedly in his/her intention, to rebirth in ecstasy, bliss, reverence and wisdom.

FOREWORD

When I think of what the phrase Divine Father means to me, my focus does not gravitate towards the spiritual realms, yet rather towards my realizations regarding my own father who raised me as a child. The interesting thing about this exquisite Divine Father book that my beloved Ivonne wrote is that she finished it right before giving birth to our first son, Iam. So in effect, I had the opportunity to read this book and experience the sutras and realizations that it invokes right after becoming a "Divine Father" myself. Thanks to her, I was able to have the most profound experience of my life and I am beyond grateful for this.

As most men will confess, there are no words that can describe becoming a father for the first time. For me this just happened 2 months ago at the age of 42, also a very important age range for men. And at the same time, I thought about my own father who raised me, who happened to have the label of "step-father", and I have had many revelations about that whole experience since I read this powerful book. When I was growing up, I thought my Dad was the worst, most strict, and generally most terrible Dad in the world, and I couldn't understand how I ended up in that family. Now that I look back on it and see all of the things he modeled to me, such as character, discipline, work ethic, honesty, and consistency, I now think of him as an enlightened master! He lived very simply and his joy was his garden where he raised all of the food that we ate. Every afternoon after work, he would put on his "work clothes", and go out and work in the garden, tilling the soil, planting seeds, or harvesting what he grew. I so much took this for granted and at the time thought he was old fashioned and stuck in his ways. He used to wake up the whole family on Saturdays at 6:00am to work in the garden, and I was the one whom he assigned the exciting and exhilarating job of pulling the weeds. I used to hate this more than anything, yet now I look back on it and see how it was training for my work now with getting people

OUT of the weeds and clearing energy blockages to them being able to GROW as human beings. It was also a great consistency practice. He was extremely focused and consistent in everything that he did and even though he didn't earn a lot of material abundance by today's standards, he saved, created, and followed a financial plan perfectly that allowed him to successfully retire very early. So I really pay tribute to him now, and wish that he was still around to see his grandson and also so that I could thank him for modeling to me what to do and what NOT to do regarding children.

This book, Divine Father, is coming out at a very important time in our history as humanity. There are not too many men around like my father anymore. They are around, yet they are not embodying their full male power as a masculine energy and behaviorally congruent. I actually see a lot of very weak men around, who choose laziness, and who choose to lie, cheat, and do not respect the divine feminine at all. This is why the male-female rift continues to this day and women have to use more of their own male energy on the planet, being the leader of the family, the provider, basically doing it all. They simply do not trust us and do not feel safe due to all of the past abuses, let downs, male dominated religions, and disrespect. This is what in my opinion this book is for. To allow men to start to truly embody their own divine masculine energy and to rebirth the qualities of impeccability, strength, vulnerability, power, honor, kindness, and grace, that are so much needed here now.

When the men embody these qualities, the women can then finally take a break, breathe a sigh of relief, and unburden themselves from playing the man's role, finally able to surrender and feel safe with their man by their side, fully supporting them. The sutras, prayers, and contemplations in this Divine Father book emit a powerful high frequency transmission that when read, melt away the shadow self of men AND women and as you read these, you will most likely feel like you are becoming more whole again. This is exactly what is happening as you are accreting light into your field and filling your mind with the ultimate divine father energy of the One Source God. This will allow you to fully embody the pure divine masculine energy of Source in a healthy way and to use this to be decisive, certain, take action, and manifest, all qualities of the original masculine energy. I am so grateful that this book is available, especially for all the men out there like me, who are or who will soon become fathers themselves. Read this book with the intention of being impeccable in every single moment and modeling to others what a strong, peaceful, loving, kind man is. I am sure that with this intention and flexible, open mind, you will become the Divine Father yourself.

Much love and respect,

Toby Alexander
Author; The Great Master
www.dnaperfection.com

INTRODUCTION

My father used to play with my brother and me in the yard. Mother would come out and say, "You're tearing up the grass." "We're not raising grass," Dad would reply. "We're raising boys." ~Harmon Killebrew

On December 11th 2009, I was hosting, teaching and attending a 5-day celebration week of T.R[2] which intention was the celebration of the Divine mother.

While in a concert of Kirtana[3], during this event, I gave a copy of my book DIVINE MOTHER, to one of my teachers and friends, Chick Moorman[4], upon receiving the book he jokingly said to me, "Hold on! This is a book of the Divine Mother and I AM the Divine father".

When he said this, as it usually happens for me when I am in his presence, something deep within me heard a call from spirit. The response to that call is this book.

As I couldn't stop thinking for the rest of the evening while in the concert of his words: I AM THE DIVINE FATHER…like an echo, those words trembled in my being very deeply.

My blood ran fast through me, tinkling in my spine, kundalini rising, I looked around and saw the masculine energy everywhere…men, women, and inside myself. For here I was, honoring the Divine Mother

---

2   Transcendental Rebirthing. www.transcendentalrebirthing.com

3   Kirtana is a singer/songwriter whose music has been described as new age vocal, devotional, "satsang," or music for awakening. Her songs celebrate divine love and investigate the truth of who we are. In addition to performing live at her own concerts, New Thought churches, and conferences, her music is used internationally by noted authors and workshop leaders in their intensives, healing seminars and satsangs around the world. www.kirtana.com

4   www.chickmoorman.com

and forgetting to honor the divine in the male. And truly, without one there is no other. Male and female are an important part of creation. Though seemingly opposites they are truly complimentary forces in the universal laws.

I thought about these all night long, and on December 12th 2009 I made a decision to write the Divine Father Book and announced it to all of my students as a way to commit myself to actually DO IT!

Within this journey I began looking at male energy in different ways.

Though I respected the energy, mentally, I began seeing the history, the struggles, the longing, the legacies, the journey the men of Earth had taken and the desperate call those in the conscious path were doing not only to us women, but also men to awaken in the support they require to be fully embraced by spirit and respected in their true gifts and strength, and their capacity to manifest peace on Earth.

I took this call from spirit not lightly, as I knew the importance of it within every cell of my being.

I have a son and a daughter and a soon to be born son, they not only are entitled but DESERVE to live in a planet of peace, of love, where safety is not something we have to fight for but that it rather springs forth from common sense as a natural happening of humanity.

As the women awaken, and the divine mother raises in its energy to rebirth humanity, men, the sacred male energy requires more support than ever.

We have no time to loose as time is of the essence.

My sons will become men one day and I desire to support them fully.

My daughter will become a woman one day, and I desire her to love herself and be strong and choose a man by her side that respects her, acknowledges her for who she is and that she has the capacity to do the same.

My planet has many children that need the support of both mother and father in harmony not in struggle…

I feel a call, I feel a NEED, and I feel it is time.

So it is, that with this urgency, I began writing this book, which is also inspired by the amazing men I have had the honor to meet while alive in this 3D. Men of impeccability in their word, of integrity, of kindness, and men that have re-birthed themselves from the shadow of unconscious realms towards worlds of light, kindness and service unto others.

This book, of course, is mainly dedicated to my own Father, a man who gifted me with a legacy of many possible choices, but mostly who modeled, the power of the mind to me.

I still have letters he wrote me when I was 7 years old. I framed one of them in my office, and it was one of my friends, who one day came to my office, read the letter, and said to me: "So you had this awareness since you were young?" I answered: What do you mean?

She said, "Look at what your father wrote to you. Most of it is the way you think today".

Evidently, her comment peaked my attention, and as I re-read again this letter from 1979, I realized the impact that my father's words had had in my choices in the present moment.

Here is a small selected excerpt of that letter on which is of most significance to me now:

May 31st, 1979

My beloved Daughter

I hope you never change!

And I wish that you always have within you, much love to give to anyone that needs it.

Dear Daughter never have bad thoughts about anyone, neither anger against anyone else.

Always, when you open your eyes in the morning, the first thing you must do is SMILE,

And think, during the whole day that you are going to be happy, with eagerness to learn, and last but not least, you will remember that your father adores you.

Your Dad & friend, Noe.

As a woman, mother, and daughter and as a female energy I invite you to use this book to pay tribute to the men in your life, your own masculine energy, and your ancestors. I invite you to forgive now and move on with grace, benevolence and determination into your next steps of greatness.

Make amends with your father if required, make amends fathers with your children, and may us all find ourselves in the divine order that by divine right we are all meant to be within the family context with no entanglements, no veils, just the divine order of love.

With deepest Gratitude & Love
Ivonne Delaflor Alexander

A hero is someone who has given his or her life to something bigger than oneself. Joseph Campbell

PART I

The Father Sutras

I am neither the mind, the intellect, nor the silent voice within; neither the eyes, the ears, the nose, nor the mouth. I am not water, fire, earth, nor ether I am Consciousness and Bliss. I am Shiva! I am Shiva! ~- Shankaracharya

Fifty-four Sutras to Master and Balance the Masculine Divine Energy Within

How to use the Sutras[5]:

The next 54 Sutras can be used during early morning meditation as a starting point of the day. The Sutras can be used randomly. And they can be used as affirmations, or you can write them in a piece of white paper and carry with you during the day. Each Sutra comes along with the author's commentary and further advises on how to use them. Most of the sutras are written as a metaphor, short poem and some use Sanskrit words.[6]

Breathe, open your mind and heart, and receive the energy transmission, which resides beyond the words. Allow the Divine Father energy to share his wisdom through your own heart. Allow your life to become a living sutra of transformation.

---

5   "Sutra" is a Sanskrit word that referred in Brahmanism to those Holy Scriptures in which all sorts of teachings and regulations were recorded. This word is not unique to Buddhism and originally meant a "line" or "string."

6   Sanskrit is the most ancient member of the European family of languages. It is an elder sister of Latin and Greek from which most of the modern European languages have been derived. The oldest preserved form of Sanskrit is referred to as Vedic . The oldest extant example of the literature of the Vedic period is the Rig-Veda . Being strictly in verse, the Rig-Veda does not give us a record of the contemporary spoken language.

The very name "Sanskrit" meant "language brought to formal perfection"

Source: http://mathormagic.com/scientists_hail_sanskrit_as_the_perfect_language

SUTRA I

Absolute Protection

Father energy, be in my presence
Male divine create through me,
Father Energy light up the darkness,
Father energy I receive thy protection now.

Commentary:

All children grow harmoniously, when they receive presence, attention and love. The Father figure gives the necessary energy transmission to the child, of protection, safety and masculine stability that grounds the energy on to Earth. Any being, of any age, strives and creates a more brilliant reality when feeling safe. Such is the importance of the Father Energy, the protector, the guardian, and the presence that tells us: that we are never alone.

Meditate upon this sutra, and visualize your own father, telling you these words. If you have no relationship with your genetical father, use this sutra to activate the skill of forgiveness, bring closure to the feelings of separation and non-safety, and embrace the divine father energy that resides in the space we all live, which is the intelligent mind of God.

SUTRA II
Non-duality of the universal spirit

Come to me, oh Non-duality, Come to me!
I invoke thee, the universal spirit!
Come to me.
Advaita, Advaita[7]! We are one!

Commentary:

When in need of Peace of mind, when daily life challenges seem to create confusion, and many decisions must be taken; meditate upon this sutra, which invokes the universal spirit to help you cut through the veils of misperception and fear, and see through the eyes of intuition guided by the heart's intelligence.

Invoke it with certainty, meditate with gratitude, and trust that what you ask is already given to you.

---

7   What is Advaita, or nonduality? Advaita means nondual or "not two." This oneness is a fundamental quality of everything. Everything is a part of and made of one nondual consciousness. www.endless-satsang.com/advaita-nonduality-oneness.htm

SUTRA III
Harmonizing light and darkness

Oh blessed mother and father thou are the Ahoratra[8],
Day, and night, as one.
Unify consciousness for the children of Earth.
Awaken the unison rhythm of this presence.
Ahoratra! Ahoratra! All one and the same.

Commentary:

When we create judgment or separation in our mind, we forget the universal principle of oneness, with this remembrance all competition disappears, Mother and Father, by the Laws of Rhythm[9], each take their place in the family system and contribute to create a harmonious manifestation. Everything has its right timing, and when we allow the dance of "what is" to flow, we create a rhythmic balance with the oneness of all and everything.

---

8   The meaning of Ahoratra is both day and night. The last three letter that is T, R, A has been taken from "HORA" a Sanskrit word that means Hour and the English word Hour has been coined from HORA. http://www.madhwas.com/aachaaravyavahara/what-is-panchangam-or-panchanga.html

9   The *law of rhythm* is another universal laws and it states that everything is moving to and fro, flowing in and out, swinging backward and forward. http://www.one-mind-one-energy.com/the-law-of-rhythm.html

SUTRA IV
Sacred Awareness for Global Organizations

Let the Akhadas[10] come, let them come. Let the wisdom of
the ancients merge. OH monks, Oh Akhadas! Remember:
celibacy is of mind. A mind One pointed to the one
within. Come to the awakening of the sacred!

Commentary:

True leadership is not only a way to serve humanity, it is also a portal
where beings like Gandhi, Mother Theresa, Jesus served the betterment
of civilization. When we are part of a community, a business or an
organization that can create change in the world, we must rise in
responsibility and focus our mind and hearts into the manifestation of
that which is good, beautiful and sustainable, we allow then wisdom that
creates win-win scenarios to emerge, we let go of EGO, and transcend
as a collective as we are focused on the good for Earth and all sentient
beings and this focus creates a collective awakening of that which truly
matters in life, and life thus is seen as sacred.

---

10 Akhada means: an organization or a wrestling arena. Mainly used here directed
to all worldwide organizations focused on betterment of the world.

SUTRA V
Manifestation of Material Prosperity

May thou Artha[11], thy sacred goal be manifested now
in the spirits of the races! May thy aim be of love, thy
artha is sacred, full of intent, living and breathing.
Awaken now, Time is of the essence.

Commentary:

There is nothing wrong with money, with prosperity or abundance. Humanity however has misinterpreted its uses and has entangled its values based on lack of priorities. So it makes sense to us that as humans we deserve to manifest and create the abundance necessary in all realms of the human experience with the aim to bring more support to the human family. With material prosperity we can contribute, we can be soul philanthropists and create major changes in a world where the laws of exchange and an economy based on earning sustenance is in place. To sustain harmony we earn and we give, we create and we share, we offer opportunities and we consistently add values to earn what we deserve. Integrity and character thus are essential to truly live beyond material prosperity, with a mental attitude of abundance with the heart one pointed towards massive contribution, starting with one self.

---

11   Artha is a Sanskrit term referring to the idea of material prosperity. In Hinduism, artha is one of the four goals of life, known as purusharthas. It is considered to be a noble goal as long as it follows the dictates of Vedic morality.

SUTRA VI

True Home

Ah! The Ashrama[12] is the residence of the heart;
the guru is in there,
look in all the rooms,
in this place he lives,
in this place he breathes.

Commentary:

There is nowhere to go, or no one to find that will rescue us from the misperceptions of suffering, or that will give us what we need in our search of enlightenment and inner peace. For eons the greatest masters have pointed the way, they have shown us that the way is within, the ultimate altar of the creator resides in ones own heart, to search for what we think will liberate us, we must first start within, as it is inside of us where the kingdom of heaven, the ashram of the soul and the human spirit reside.

---

12 The word Ashram describes a house where a true Guru is living and teaching God-seekers seeking spiritual advice and help. An Ashram always is free of any religion and open to absolutely all. http://www.kriyayoga.com/english/encyclopedia/ashram.htm

SUTRA VII
Residing in the Heart

Thy Atman[13] is residing n thy heart,
The inner child is nothing but the inner self.
Come to play in this majestic field.
Play and rely on his grace, and rest in his arms.

Commentary:

Growing up seems to be a veil for the joy that it is to be human, the indoctrinations, domestications and belief systems we all grow up with, seem but to rust the remembrance of our true delight of life, the joy of being…when we remember that we are not our thoughts, that we are not what we believe in, we then allow the inner child to play again, to shine through our eyes and allow the ebb and flow of the river of life to move, we splash in the water, we then play with the rain, we awaken, YES, we awaken from the dream given to us and start dreaming again, anew, fresh, like a child, free of fear and full of wonder, where our soul delights in its own grace.

---

13 Atman in Hinduism is that core of life in absence of which the existence of the body itself gets negated. Atman in Hinduism stands for our soul, which resides in the heart within the body. For that matter… every single living being… be it the form of an insect, plant or an animal… the presence of atman is a confirmed fact. http://www. godrealized.com/define_atman.html

SUTRA VIII
Embodiment of Devotion

Oh father! Thy bhakti[14] is the devotion I see of thy love in me.
My devotion is yours, as I see salvation from misperceptions
within your reality.

Commentary:

Men are taught at a young age not to cry, to swallow up something, that was considered as weakness, or only for girls; emotions. There is nothing more powerful than the devotional energy of the divine masculine, when we allow emotions to turn into devotion, we heal aspects of life where we repressed what we thought will put us on a vulnerable position. We discover then that vulnerability is power, and that we no longer need to move in life based on fight or flight, but in the center of these two motions, where ewe are grounded, balance and whole, and where we allow love from the masculine energy to access our hearts and thus feel the strength of a well anchored tree, and we also remain flexible as we allow devotion to permeate our mind and spirit.

---

14   Bhakti is a path to achieving salvation through loving devotion to a particular deity, open to all persons irrespective of sex or caste.

SUTRA IX
Indestructible Wisdom

Father, in thee I found the power of indestructible wisdom. The highest level of modeling that any life form can reach, resides in thy kindness and gentle strength. All divinity exists in your presence.

Commentary:

We must be reverent to the masculine power within all beings, without the Father; there is no life, and its image and modeling set the tone for its children future choices. The Father energy, his actions, and applied wisdom, becomes the book of law that his children will obey with loyalty and love. There is nothing more powerful than gentleness, and the divine father knows well how to give this to his children. We must just allow ourselves to feel this, and remember that what we model, is what we leave in our humanity as a footprint for the next generations.

SUTRA X
Power of Creation

Father; you have been conceived chiefly as a member of the triad of power of creation. God as Mother, God as Father, and God as Spirit. Within your existence, all souls exist in blissful contemplation.

Commentary:

The divine trinity resides in us all, as we all contain the aspects of father, mother and child. When we contemplate this sutra w are reminded to acknowledge these powers with us and to bring them to balance, allowing them to do each their work, without judgment and separation, and use these forces within us, to create a reality of love, peace and brilliant manifestations. This sutra also helps us remember that we are all created from a trinity energetic field, thus we can have more compassion and cease all judgment as we acknowledge that the power of creation resides in all beings.

SUTRA XI
Whole Acceptance

Divine names of thee, Oh masculine principle! Sometimes a child, sometimes a young boy, and sometimes a man. I raise my spirit as a signature energy that accepts all that is you as one.

Commentary:

Judging the male energy is a hopeless war with reality. The male, as well as the female, can be manifested in many different ages, times and faces. Allow it to be what it is. This sutra is helpful when you expect the male energy to be a "limited something". To be perfect all the time is an exhausting belief. Perfection resides in the acceptance of what is.

SUTRA XII

Sweet Surrender

Thy heart, mind, soul and spirit rejoice in their masculine
power. Oh how sweet it is thy surrender in to the
arms of the Mother. There in the man is born.

Commentary:

A True man knows how to respect and surrender to the divine feminine
energy, especially to its own feminine energy that resides in his gentleness,
kindness and even in his strength.

To be open, to embrace the wholeness of being, merges the energies
of the masculine and the feminine, creating with this a wholeness, a
divine essence field, where the man is born in to its own power, its own
gentle warriorship nature.

SUTRA XIII
The force of Creation

In thy divine choices reside the sacred principles of "Dhana"
the divine generosity of action, giving as a force of creation.

Commentary:

Action is male energy by nature, and when we add to it generosity, and
an intention of giving and contributing, this force becomes a major fuel
of manifestation for the betterment of self and humanity. So go ahead,
use this sutra to propel you to act upon the roots and force of a giving,
loving, generous heart.

SUTRA XIV
Masculine Cells

Father Energy, the Dharma[15] of thy love is in my cells reverberating as my own actions, and the righteous duty of thy heart is in me.

Commentary:

The Father energy is to keep the balance, and the safety by nature. It protects its family, its community, and its world. It's pure warrior energy in motion. With this sutra you may desire to invoke this principle within you when you feel out of balance or feel the need for the sense of safety back in to your life. Visualize your cells reverberating with this divine protection, and know that you are finally safe by being present, here and now.

---

15   *that which upholds, supports or maintains* <u>*the regulatory order of the universe*</u>
Source: http://en.wikipedia.org/wiki/Dharma

SUTRA XV
Benevolence

The monkhood of thy spirit breathes and swim in my
blood through benevolent actions, and through this
I protect, I observe, I watch, I take action.

Commentary:

All beings have both feminine and masculine energy. When we learn
to use these polarities wisely, we then can tap in an unlimited source
of personal power that can be used as a force for good. This sutra is
a metaphor of what the robe of a monk represents for the masculine
energy. Reminding us of the power in vulnerability, humility and non-
violence, as we take action in life with our awakened masculine energy.

SUTRA XVI
Sacred Geometry

Thy life and actions manifest the sacred geometrical[16] formula for all life. Thine is the eternal responsibility of modeling what is good for the species. I thank you.

Commentary:

Every action we take, thought we make, words we say, or feelings we choose to express create in the space a resonance that impact the collective in an instantaneous way. We are all, as we speak, creating a sacred geometrical vibration from our choices all of the time, thus the importance to be aware of the responsibility this conveys as we impact our world and create ripples of cause and effect wherever we are that impact the future generations in the here and now.

---

16   Sacred geometry is the geometry used in the planning and construction of religious structures such as churches, temples, mosques, religious monuments, altars, and tabernacles; as well as for sacred spaces such as temenoi, sacred groves, village greens and holy wells, and the creation of religious art. However, in sacred geometry, symbolic and sacred meanings are ascribed to certain geometric shapes, and certain geometric proportions.

SUTRA XVII

Heart Atonement

Father, thou are for my eyes, my Istadevata[17] My heart
is tuned to thee, and all of my attention is focused
in the integrity of thy thoughts and actions.

Commentary:

What we choose to admire in others, most likely is a quality we already
have in ourselves. When we follow our role models, we will embrace and
embody the traits and skills they teach us by their actions, thoughts,
and deeds. Thus is important to be aware of our own integrity, our own
power of choice and to become a role model of impeccable character,
and benevolence. To see the good in all, and to make the choice to use
those learned skills for the benefit of mankind and the journey of self-
realization.

---

17   Sanskrit word meaning Cherished or chosen Deity.

SUTRA XVIII
Importance of Meditation

Oh Divine masculine, it is through your consistency
practice, and Jnana[18] that I move forward and confident in
my own spiritual practice, I shall follow in these steps.

Commentary:

To have a clear mind, vibrating in stillness is essential as we walk the
steps forward in to the creation of our own reality. As our fathers and
ancestors left their footprints that guide us all in to a new path for us
to continue creating a humanity of love, we remain committed to honor
them by carrying within our mind and hearts the power of consistency
and the mastery of practice and meditation. Confidence thus, is an
inevitable outcome, when with serenity, and peace of mind we walk the
path of light that our fathers walked before us.

---

18   Sanskrit word meaning Knowledge acquired through meditation and study as a
means of reaching Brahman

SUTRA XIX
Creation and Destruction

Oh ancestors of the male lineage, we have created and
destroy each Kalpa[19] there is a new opportunity, the
choice now through thy power is a creation of the values of
universal truth. Birth and rebirth reside in this choice.

Commentary:

Every moment while alive is a new opportunity to recreate ourselves
a new. The past doesn't determine our future. It is our choices, our
commitment and our will power, which will drive us to move forward
making better choices each and every moment. Bettering ourselves, our
community and our world, as we choose to birth ourselves back in to
luminosity empowered by clear values aligned with the universal aspects
of truth.

---

19   One of the Brahmanic eons, a period of 4,320,000,000 years. At the end of each
Kalpa the world is annihilated

SUTRA XX
The radiant Sun

Male power, that feeds my soul, and gives life to all sentient creatures,
I bow to thee, oh Kama[20], thou golden power resides in me.

Commentary:

The importance of honoring our fathers is essential to move in life with
ease, gratitude and reverence to our own divinity. We are born from our
fathers and mothers, we owe them respect and the choice to live our lives
with honor, grace and stability. By doing this, we honor the source of our
primordial life, and we thus awaken within, the male father aspect within
our souls and mind.

---

20 Sanskrit word Kama- meaning The golden one

SUTRA XXI
Divine Destiny

Thy karma[21] is inherited by all our next generations, the destiny
determined by it. Father, may it be love the legacy, may it be
joy the living breath for the continuation of the species

Commentary:

Whatever we do, say or think, it's shared with the collective, where we
either choose to support or pollute. It is of foremost importance that our
whole being is aligned with the great integrity, as this is what our future
generations will inherit and that which will feed their offspring as well.
So to do what is right, is investing in enriching the creation of brilliant
future for all sentient beings.

---

21   Karma Sanskrit word meaning- The total effect of a person's actions and conduct
during the successive phases of the person's existence, regarded as determining the
person's destiny

SUTRA XXII
The Compassionate One

Fear not, the fact that others who are blinded by their own karmic path may not see you; yet, God never dismisses thy compassion.

Commentary:

The thirst of humanity to be seen and appreciated sometimes becomes a burden towards the path of self-realization. When contemplating this sutra, it may be time to release an expectation to be seen, heard by another person, and start looking within, and remember that for the eternal presence of the Divine Father, you are always taken care for, you are always seen and heard, you are never alone.

SUTRA XXIII

Fear Soother

Thy keerthana[22] is the soothing breeze for all my fears, thy words and presence are the katha[23] that I listen and observe.

Commentary:

There is power in sound, in the voice, in the song of creation. The voice of father is a soothing chant for the child. It sings of stability, safety and protection. It commands respect, it uplifts, motivates, it loves. Listen to this voice within, and chant its tune with the stillness that comes from being willing to listen for the Father's chant as the voice of thunder in creation.

---

22 Sanskrit word Keerthanas- Is a devotional songs. Normally sung in groups

23 Sanskrit word Katha- Religious discourses involving Ramayana, Bhagavatgeetha, Srimad Bhagavathgeetha

SUTRA XXIV
Harvest

The kharmapala[24] of the masculine love will be seen in
the faces of all children smiling and acting upon universal
values with determination, honesty and love

Commentary:

To be focused on merit and integrity is a force that will become the
fuel for future generations to live a life of grace. The Father impact on
his children is such, that his actions must be dampened with absolute
stability and love. To love is to have limitless power, and this is the
pristine essence of the Father. Bathe in this love.

---

24   Sanskrit word Kharmapala- The benefits or merits of one`s action

SUTRA XXV
Purification of Sin

It is love, kindness and serenity the ultimate festival for clearing and purifying the mind body and spirit, Oh Father! How powerful is thy sacredness, a true Khumba Mela[25] of the inner realms, and how benevolent the celebration in thy heart.

Commentary:

To celebrate masculine energy, is essential as part of being human. Masculine energy, Father Energy, is a gift that must be celebrated and acknowledged. To realize the blessing it is of this energy polarity, is to create a celebration of this aspect of creation.

---

25 Sanskrit word referring to a Hindu festival held once every twelve years in one of four sacred sites, where bathing for purification from sin is considered especially efficacious

SUTRA XXVI
The Power of Thought

Father energy, thy thoughts and words are Ksherasagara[26]
for me, they are a vast ocean of milk, which feeds and
nurtures my growth. For as you share, I become.

Commentary:

The Right word has the power to trigger bountiful emotions and trigger higher states of being. Our Father's words become like commands to our soul, thus we learn, behave and create belief systems based in the shared words of our Father, spoken or unspoken. The thoughts that emanate from words, and vice versa, when used with purpose, consciousness and love, become the powerful tools for manifesting an ocean of possibilities towards the journey of the remembrance of the **I AM** presence.

---

26 Sanskrit word, kshera=milk. Sagara= Ocean

SUTRA XXVII
Letting Go

I am thy beloved daughter, thy beloved son; let me go with
blessings from thy world, as I create with great love for thee love
a new kshetra[27], a new universe, and interdependent world.

Commentary:

To cut the cords, and to create our life as unique, independently of our
Father, it is a gift and a way of honoring this sacred energy. Many people
think they have to be exactly the same as the father and that choosing
to be differently may be a betrayal. To create our own identity and take
flight in to our own gifts creates a sacred field of love which in return
creates a sacred reverence for our Father, as we pay tribute and gratitude
for the gifts his energy gave us to take flight in to our own creation.

---

27   Sanskrit word meaning Kshetra- Planet in its own sign

SUTRA XXVIII
Single Steps

Like a sacred kyrma[28], you walk the path of the great ones
before you. Male energy, I say to thee, awaken to the sacredness
of each single step. Rush not to the shore of manifestation.

Commentary:

To be masculine, or to use our masculine energy is usually applied for
action. Most of the times this action needs to be done quickly, or we
think it needs to be done right away. To truly use masculine energy in
its wise form, we must remember that to pause, to practice patience and
to breathe in each step we take in life to accomplish something, doesn't
mean we wont get there, or we get there later, in truth these are tools that
gives us more energy to take each step even stronger and aim towards the
goal of accomplishment and manifestation of our desires.

---

28   Sanskrit word meaning tortoise or turttle

SUTRA XXIX
New Beginning

Ah father, each magha[29] I will connect to thee. In
the sacred numerology of mastery we shall meet, we
will refresh our connection and rebirth in
a new beginning.

Commentary:

There is not such thing as an "It's too late for..." anything, if we need healing or reconnection with our Father or our own masculine energy, there is always the possibility of a new beginning, a new opportunity, here symbolized as the first month of a year, as a metaphor of starting a new.

We always have this possibility, to let go of the past, and start anew, fresh, present, and move forward with generosity, taking with us the learned lessons and the positive gifts and meaning we gave to each experience along the way.

---

29 Magha- The eleventh month of the Hindu calendar; corresponds to January in the Gregorian calendar

SUTRA XXX
Liberation

I pray for the liberation of thy spirit, of my own. Blessed be
the moment thy heart was created in Moksha[30], where I find
the place to return back home, my immortal journey.

Commentary:

Being free from any type of slavery from beliefs, assumptions, and
judgments brings us the experience not only true liberation but also the
capacity to be present, in the moment, and enrich our presence towards
ourselves and other human beings. The Heart is always in the Now, and
when we approach existence with this awareness we become immortal,
present, right here and right now. When our fathers love us with presence,
they give us a gift that transcends time, it is a life that is eternal, that
feeds our souls beyond the concept of time, and that motivates us to do
the same with our children, and anyone we encounter.

True liberation resides in giving and allowing freedom to be...to
simply be.

---

30 Moksha- Emancipation of the soul from rebirth

SUTRA XXXI
Noble Strength

Mandara[31] of my spirit, thou are the immensity of support that resides in thy image and essence. I praise the nature of thy noble strength

Commentary:

For any child, his father is the foundation of his life, the strength, the image of power, of stability, and support. When a father has character, values and lives by ethics and sacred principles, the modeling he gives by these, motivates the child to grow as a noble tree would. With rectitude, right attitude and solidity. Elegance and power merge, and the essence of safety and being, radiates effortlessly when we have such support.

This is true noble strength.

---

31 Mandara- Is the holy mountain which is the center of the world

SUTRA XXXII
Pillar of creation

Oh sacred male one, without thee the mother cant hold strongly the pillar of her responsibility, hold yours with honor and courage and then hers will rise and birth will take place harmoniously

Commentary:

The importance of the father support for the Mother, the male for the female, is essential for any child to strive in life. When the masculine supports the feminine and vice versa, their offspring of love takes flight as an emissary of balance and congruency, so much needed these days in humanity. When choosing to study this sutra, remember to bring balance and acceptance to both the male and female aspect of your being. Treat all beings with respect, and love one another. Support with this, the future generations in the now.

SUTRA XXXIII
Nirvana

My nirvana[32] resides in the solid steps of my mother and father,
and in me the responsibility to use these steps wisely.

Commentary:

Even though most of our habits and fate are determined by the legacies of our parents, we can step up any hidden hindrances by the power of taking responsibility of our creation. When we do this, the past liberates itself from us, the future becomes an open brilliant door, while we remain, present, actualized and ready to live in the here, and now, with ease, grace, and consciousness.

---

32 Nirvana- Emancipation from ignorance and the extinction of all attachment

SUTRA XXXIV
Infinite Sky

Where thy actions are, my soul follows. May it be that thy
heaven and astronomy of thy life is one of the paths of the
noble ones. I reach for the infinite sky in thy heaven

Commentary:

To be a role model is a great power and responsibility. We must raise
our thoughts, actions and words to the heights of the human ethic of
spiritual beauty. Our aim must be to become that which we wish to see
in the world. The sky is an open vessel of possibilities, and when we reach
beyond the stars to attain self-realization, we then commit to lead by
example and share by our own integrity the truth of what being present
truly is. May your modeling be such that he/she who follows you attains
self-liberation in joy.

SUTRA XXXV

Actions

Preach me not with thy spoken words only, but with thy actions filled with certainty and love, these will become my eternal Pravachana[33]

Commentary:

Once again, this sutra shows us that we must act in accordance to a field of integrity and wholeness. To say one thing and do another is not only a discrepancy in the fields of living but also a transgression towards the universal laws of cause and effect. We must embrace and embody congruency and integrity in absolutely all areas of our being. Not a single spec of dust within shall remain untouched by this wholeness. Then, and only then you have earned the right to teach, not by words, but by who you are, silent, present, in the here and now.

---

33 Religious discourses

SUTRA XXXVI
Divine Absorption

Oh male force, the fuel for Samadhi[34], the power of will resides in
the success of my desired manifestations, model this accordingly,
and we shall be absorbed in the vast realm of consciousness

Commentary:

One more time, the masculine energy, the action taker, the warrior force
field, here is represented as a metaphor of the power of Will, a power
such that can create, transmute, destroy and bring in to manifestation
any desire outcome. To increase will power, is to increase inner strength
and the commitment towards reality to manifest conscious awakening
by relentless focus, meditation and divine discipline.

---

34 State of intense concentration or absorption of consciousness, the product of
meditation. In Hinduism, it is achieved through Yoga, in which the consciousness is
absorbed in the object of meditation. In Buddhism, samadhi is the result of mind-
development as distinct from insight-development (see vipassana), and is attainable by
non-Buddhists as well as Buddhists. In Zen Buddhism, samadhi allows the meditator
to overcome dualistic subject-object awareness through unity with the object of
meditation.

SUTRA XXXVII
Devotional Offering

I offer you my heart in freedom. Free of attachments
and entanglements I love you. Oh father, what I learned
from you I offer it to the Puja[35] of your soul.

Commentary:

To be grateful is to praise the law of Love. To realize that any experience, any teaching and learning has been a gift towards our soul in this human experience, is to realize that every moment in creation is benevolent, every experience sacred, every being we meet, a teacher in the school of life. A Thankful heart, thus, merges in the beatitude of gratitude, where divine humility is born, and the temple of life is now approached as sacred.

---

35 Puja- Daily devotion consisting of a ritual offering of food, drink, and ritual actions and prayers, most commonly to an image of a deity

SUTRA XXXVIII
Religious Silence

Father, thy silence is a religious ritual where I learn where to reside in my self. Sacred silence without internal chatter makes me feel like a pundit[36], officiating a ritual of modeling to my next generations.

Commentary:

The Power of silence is seen not only as needed for any true spiritual seeker, but also to open the gateways to the inner world where the true master can be met. To offer silence of mind to our self is to create peace within and bridge this to the world. Inner silence is the force where all creation emanates, where all fear dies, where enlightenment takes place.

---

36   Pundits- Is a Brahmin who officiates religious hindu rituals

SUTRA XXXIX
Good Merit

The mere desire for Punya[37] to take place for all my existence
is not strong enough, we must add the action of spirit, and
the determination that the male single pointed focus can
bring for this manifestation of good merits for all.

Commentary:

Wishing is not enough, dreaming is not enough, thinking is not enough,
we must act accordingly, and we must take action, move forward, and
work with determined purpose to manifest our inner higher desires.
If we wish to attract good, we must do good, if we wish to attract love,
we must love others, if we wish to manifest self-realization, we must
meditate. Good actions birth Good results. It is as simple as that.

---

37   Punya- Good karma, or merit, accumulated from good actions

SUTRA XL
Recognition of Truth

Thou are not a legend, but a reality. I breathe thanks
to the electric and magnetic field of my mother and
father. I recognize and embrace this truth.

Commentary:

To honor our Mother and Father is to honor God. To realize that we
have been born from the forces of creation is to surrender to the power
of truth. We are oneness in the ocean of diversity, and when the energies
of masculine and feminine embrace, they birth us as the One source
consciousness of eternity.

SUTRA XLI
Leadership

Thou are the leader of the unit call family. I vow to love and be loyal to the teachings you bring forth as a leader. Choose wisely what you teach, as I will follow with absolute determination.

Commentary:

Leadership is an act from the heart, and the acts that come from this space generate an empowering model that many follow. It is important that we bring impeccability in our thoughts and actions, especially when we know that the steps we take today, may be the guiding lights for the steps our children may choose to take tomorrow.

SUTRA XLII
Unspoken Strength

In thy heart resides the mystery of the unspoken strength,
the wounds of the ancestors and the heroic journey of the
species. Rise and share its voice with Passion and love.

Commentary:

There is nothing in the history of man that is wrong. All the past
experiences, all the wounds, the hidden battles and struggles, create a
field where heroes are born, where rising like the phoenix does from the
ashes, is not only possible but a real experience for he/she who keeps
moving forward honoring the past and all experiences, and becoming
a vessel of strength and hope for others in the path of the Hero. Being
alive, by itself, is a true heroic journey.

SUTRA XLIII
Vulnerability

I rejoice in the vulnerability of a heart open for service, I
walk the path of the wise ones, I protect the female energy,
and I am one with the male principle of creation.

Commentary:

A true warrior's call is an invocation of true honor, the embodiment of
benevolent character, wearing the armor of integrity. Within this call,
the true man knows that vulnerability is power, and the noble acts he
performs are not a weakness revealed, but a strength gained.

SUTRA XLXIV
Alchemy of love

Thy command has the power to turn ocean waters in to milk fountains. Use this power wisely of Father! The Alchemy of thy love is endless

Commentary:

Power carries the power of responsibility. When we have raised our frequencies and our mind to more mastery, we grow in the field of moral authority, not to control, manipulate or abuse others, but to allow wisdom and kindness to use these gifts for the benefit of mankind and not against it.

SUTRA XLV
Heart traditions

Inherit me the abundant fortune of thy heart. May
this be a sacred sampradaya[38] that is shared through
the heart of the cosmology of the male energy

Commentary:

The power of rituals and traditions is a gift we create for our families
and future generations. It gives us a sense of sacredness and holiness,
it reminds us of our divine essence, and if we do a ritual out of loving
one another, of treating each other with respect, of acknowledging the
non violent powers of the masculine energy, we are surely in the path of
awakening, and most of all the path of an open heart.

---

38 Sampradaya- Tradition

SUTRA XLVI
Heroic Journey

I am eternally watching the forces within thee. Oh master
of warrior ship, may the battle be within, and may the
heroic journey reside in the leaping of all obstacles within
the darkness of ones soul conquering the self with love

Commentary:

The enemy is never outside oneself, it is within. Any battle towards
another, its a reflection of the wars within each of us. We must bring
peace within by knowing oneself. Through meditation, discipline and
commitment to the now and do what is right, we leap all obstacles, we
arrive to our destiny, the surrender of the ego, the awakening of self-
love.

SUTRA XLVII
Will Power

The power of thy will resides in your embodiment of
truth. Father, guide me gently towards the realization
of my being. Fill your basic needs with kind acts.

Commentary:

We can attain liberation in many ways, through suffering, or through
simply being present here and now. We can learn lessons by immediate
karma of our actions when they are out of alignment of source, or attain
wisdom by meditating, learning, applying and empowering our will. Both
paths are a choice, leading to the same ocean of truth eventually. Yet the
choice to embody this through kindness and peace is always possible…
it's a personal choice in our path … the path of enlightenment.

SUTRA XLVIII
Divine Service

The Seva[39] of thy work will pass on a ripple of modeling and sacred continuation. To serve is divine; to be humble in the service is the nature of God and the true strength of man.

Commentary:

Service is the language of the divine, those who have the opportunity to support, assist others, and support others in any or all areas of life, are beyond privileged for the experience of being. There's no higher aim for enlightenment but this: to be of service.

---

39   Seva- Service or to serve

SUTRA XLVIX
Faith

Male beliefs, transmute into gold, sacred thoughts shift in
to clear perception, have shraddha[40] in your heart.

Commentary:

Anything we belief in we create as a reality. To empower thoughts that
generate beliefs that can generate a force for good is a gift we can give
to others and ourselves. To change our perception when needed, or
to give positive meanings to all situations, is to become the ultimate
alchemist where all charcoal becomes a polished diamond, the symbol
of the enlightened mind and the awakened heart.

---

40   Shraddha- Faith; belief

SUTRA L
Alignment

Thy words, thoughts, and actions must be aligned
with God Head consciousness. Praise on love, act on
love and think of love, this is enlightenment

Commentary:

Simple, the focus here is to become love for the sake of love, without the need of an external force to "give it to us". We are the generators of this ultimate law, the divine path of the ancients, and the ancestors of light. We are the love of the eternal, we are love as a soul, and our fate is love.

SUTRA LI
Ethics of the Divine

Force nothing by rigidity, create everything through flexibility. Ethics are the power tools for the true master. Values as priorities the fuel.

Commentary:

That what you do most of the time, is what you value the most. To have in order our higher values based on love, contribution, and growth, is to create fields of love and become gardeners of ascended souls and spirits. To flow, to embrace, to trust, and be open to existence, is the lesson that nature gives us and where, if we choose to learn from it and act upon it, we become the power of the immovable, the divine, the eternal and the now. With clear priorities we can embrace everything in its wholeness, and by doing this, we become THE ONE.

SUTRA LII
Individuation of the Divine

My consciousness is individuation of the divine. Reject nothing that differs from thy point of view. Embrace all differences, mistakes and failures as stepping-stones of strength to build and rebuild civilization.

Commentary:

To be open to feedback, to embrace mistakes as learning opportunity, to drop prejudice of things, events, and others, and to choose instead to be all-inclusive, facilitates the process of godhead realization and inner remembrance of the powers of creation within. Nothing is against you, all is in your favor, given to you to awaken you, support you, empower you, and embrace you. Love is all-inclusive.

SUTRA LIII
Embracing the Male Power

Observe thy soul with eager stability. Master thy emotions
with joyful embrace. Respect all feminine nature with words,
acts and thoughts. Embrace with this thy own male power.

Commentary:

The powerful male treats the feminine with absolute reverence and
respect. To treat her other than this is an act of violence. Excuses and
justifications on why this must be done are but hopeless loops of karmic
ties. A true warrior has benevolence, and guardianship inner sense of
the feminine. He recognizes she is his own soul, thus he respects her as
sacred, as the mother, as the lover, and by doing this he embodies more
of his own divinity as a male, creating with this the perfect balance of
the yin and yang.[41]

---

41   (in Chinese philosophy) the passive female principle of the universe, characterized
as female and sustaining and associated with earth, dark, and cold. Contrasted with
yang. ORIGIN from Chinese yīn 'feminine,' 'moon,' 'shade.'. (in Chinese philosophy)
the active male principle of the universe, characterized as male and creative and
associated with heaven, heat, and light. Contrasted with yin.
ORIGIN from Chinese yáng 'male genitals,' 'sun,' 'positive.'

SUTRA LIV
The True Renunciation

As male power we abandon the attachment to all fruits of
actions, with an inner detachment focused in meditation,
sincerity and absolute surrender to the will of God. We keep
our word. We renounce to the falsehood of the Maya[42].

Commentary:

To surrender to what is, dropping all judgments, wants and needs is to
open up to the gateway of infinity. We begin to see clearly and with a
kind mind, the reality of the divine, benevolent, loving and ever present
creation. We surrender our ego, our sense of self, our identities, our
righteousness, we then, and only through surrender and resisting nothing
we truly become the I AM presence, that needs no more labels, no more
stories, no more praise, just the isness of being I AM.

---

42   In Hinduism, a powerful force that creates the cosmic illusion that the phenomenal
world is real. The word maya originally referred to the wizardry with which a god can
make human beings believe in what turns out to be an illusion, and its philosophical
sense is an extension of this meaning. The concept is especially important in the
Advaita School of the orthodox system of Vedanta, which sees maya as the cosmic
force that presents the infinite Brahman as the finite phenomenal world.

PART II

Daily Prayers

'PRAYER is not asking. It is a longing of the soul. It is daily admission of one's weakness. It is better in prayer to have a heart without words than words without a heart.' Gandhi

Daily Prayers

Revelation Is worthless without Action- Byron Katie

This section of the book is a transitional space after studying and applying the sutras in your life. In the next pages you will find a prayer for each day of the week. It is suggested you read the prayer of the day, upon awakening and before going to sleep. It is extremely important to always begin and complete prayers with the words: "Thank you". And realize that the true daily prayer you can live, are the actions you take and embrace during the day. They are also good closings after studying the Divine Father Sutras.

MONDAY PRAYER

'WHEN one is praying in a room, he is not alone, he is there with God, then to him God is not in the highest, heaven, but close to him, before him, in him.... all names and forms disappear before Him. Then every word of, prayer, he utters is a living word....'Unknown

I pray today for my male energy to act upon deeds of certainty and kindness.

I pray to respect all beings and increase with this my self-esteem and self worth.

I act upon love and determination.

I am love.

Thank You...

TUESDAY PRAYER

'MAN often thinks that, as God is the knower of the heart, there can be no need of any recital or gesture in prayer: but that it would surely be sufficient if he were to sit in the silence and think of God. But this is not so; it is according to the extent of a man's consciousness of prayer that his prayer reaches God.' ~ Unknown

Today I pray for inner silence to calm the waves of the mind.

I pray for all my beliefs to be actualized in brilliancy and love

And I pray to restore my true divine essence aligned with the Divine Father Support.

Thank You

WEDNESDAY PRAYER

'MAN asks another question as to why God, who knows already what he wants and what is the need of his life, should require to be asked at all. For answer to this we have the words of Christ ' Ask and ye shall receive, knock and it shall be opened unto you'. In another words, this means that though God knows your need, it has to become clear and definite to yourself by prayer.' ~ Unknown

I pray today to embrace and remember that what I ask for is always given.

I pray to see the manifestation of this truth with my heart and eyes.

I pray so that all beings ask for that which benefits humanity.

I pray to contribute to the abundance that I receive.

Thank You

THURSDAY PRAYER

'The question whether God has time to give attention to our prayer is answered by the mystics, who says that it is through the medium of man himself that God hears his prayers.' ~ Unknown

Today I pray to ask in abundance of my deepest desires,

I ask brilliantly and truthfully,

I ask with passion and gratitude.

I pray to remain consistent with my focus and meditations.

I pray to see the light in the path that I choose to create and become one with it.

Thank You

FRIDAY PRAYER

'The ignorant believer, by his claim of BELIEF, causes a revolt in an intelligent person, thereby turning him into an unbeliever. Parents think nowadays that by giving the children the belief that has been held in the family, they make them narrow, yet at the same time have no substitute, no belief and it is very difficult to believe later on. ~ Unknown

I pray today to respect and embrace the individuated consciousness of all beings, to remain free of desires to control and manipulate others, I pray to embrace diversity and respect the uniqueness of the whole of creation, and with this I pray to embody my own uniqueness.

Thank You

SATURDAY PRAYER

'It is something living in the soul, in the mind, and in the heart of a man- it is absence keeps man as dead, and its presence gives him life. If there is any RELIGION, it is this. Unknown

I pray today to be present and remain with awakened presence, to detach from false perception and to live within the sacred religion that love is. I pray to attract all love and abundance, and become this love that I ask for as well.

Thank You

SUNDAY PRAYER

*'When you call yourself an Indian or a Muslim or a Christian
or a European, or anything else, you are being violent. Do you
see why it is violent? Because you are separating yourself from
the rest of mankind. When you separate yourself by belief, by
nationality, by tradition, it breeds violence. So a man who is
seeking to understand violence does not belong to any country,
to any religion, to any political party or partial system; he is
concerned with the total understanding of mankind ~Krishnamurti*

I pray today to be free of labels, and to see everything and everyone as holy,

I pray to remain boundless of titles, names and identifications.

Today I pray for non-violence within me, and to receive higher understanding that only an open heart aligned with a flexible mind can receive. I pray today to behold goodness in all.

Thank You

PART III

Monthly Contemplations for Manifestation of Spiritual Greatness

'Tenderness and kindness are not signs of weakness and despair, but manifestations of strength and resolution'. Kahlil Gibran

Monthly Contemplations for Manifestation of Spiritual Greatness

In this section, the contemplations are to be used at the beginning of each month to have a one focused pointed intent, and a higher spiritual goal to manifest a higher frequency vibrational month, with brilliance and greatness. Each month also includes a suggested breathing visualization to anchor even deeper the greatness you desire to manifest.

It is suggested you read it the first day of the month, three times per day, and read again when in need to remember your intention. The Prayers and Sutras are warming up stages for this chapter that is aimed to increase the clarity of your intention.

For remember: Intention is vested with power.

JANUARY

I visualize this month being showered buy golden light frequencies, with the intention to remain assertive, kind and productive.

I relinquish all excuses, self-diminishment and lack of confidence. I embrace sacred beginnings and walk these with firm steps of reverence.

I breathe in the light of the masculine power and exhale any doubts, I breathe in the support of the elementals, and exhale fear, I breathe in love, I exhale Joy.

FEBRUARY

For this month I shall receive more and more from the eternal abundance wealth of universal nature. I am open to receive, as I visualize gateways of light opening within me. I affirm each day of this month the power of love inside of me that radiates from within to the whole.

I breathe in enthusiasm for living, I exhale hesitation, I breathe in trust, I exhale all doubts, I breathe in joy, and I exhale love.

MARCH

This month I welcome the spring of my soul. I focus on creativity, creation and empowerment. I affirm that wholeness is my destiny in the now.

I breathe in the commitment to live in congruency with my divine nature, I exhale misperceptions and false projections, I breathe in commitment for life, I exhale outdated belief systems, I breathe in love, I exhale joy.

APRIL

I open up my heart and mind and attune them both with the oneness of ascended love-filled frequencies. I am the eternal manifestation of the divine and this month I walk in humbleness and humility my path of purpose and mission.

I breathe in simplicity, exhale complexity, I breathe in love, I exhale joy.

MAY

This month I set my intent to be attuned with the Divine Father's power. Where I receive all support and walk steady and consistently my path of success. I respect all living forms and all genders. I embrace the goodness of the nature of reality.

I breathe in acceptance of what is, exhale all complaints, I breathe in success, exhale all failure, I breathe in opportunities, I exhale disappointments, I breathe in love, I exhale joy.

JUNE

This month I remember that mind is a tool for creation. Reason has a right to exist and I am no one to judge another one. I commit to recognize this month that all my fellow human beings are in the same path of awakening higher consciousness, and commit to move beyond reason and logic in to a place of emotional mastery and a balanced acceptance of all as it is.

I breathe in totality, exhale fragmentation, I breathe in faith, exhale mind disturbances, I breathe in oneness, exhale separation, I breathe in love, I exhale joy.

JULY

This month I commit to embrace all higher aspirations of my soul, I remain constant and sincere, and commit to master my will-power to remember that the Divine alone in me, is enough for me to receive all what I desire and need. I keep moving forward.

I breathe in movement, exhale stagnation, I breathe in intention, I exhale hesitation, I breathe in certainty, I exhale emotional discomforts, I breathe in love, I exhale joy.

AUGUST

This month I will remain conscious and aware of my own soul, I commit to know myself deeper and love myself wisely. I will be aware of any identification I choose to make with the mental manifestation. I will remain true to my soul.

I breathe in soul power, I exhale mental identification, I breathe in ecstasy, I exhale pessimism, I breathe in motivation, I exhale deception, I breathe in love, and I exhale joy.

SEPTEMBER

This month I commit to remember that within me resides all possible strength, I lift the veils within my perception and invest time with nature, I live clear with my priorities in order and uplift myself with higher values. I live in love, and shed what is not needed any more in peaceful ways.

I breathe in readiness, I exhale fear of making mistakes, I inhale stepping up, I exhale the path of least resistance, I breathe in love, and I exhale joy.

OCTOBER

This month I commit to expand myself in love beyond concepts and ideas. I will liberate others and myself from attachments and unnecessary bonds. I allow love to be the moving sea that it is. I flow effortlessly.

I inhale love, I exhale hatred, I inhale forgiveness, I exhale holding on to the past, I breathe in self-acceptance, I exhale judgments, I breathe in love, I exhale joy.

NOVEMBER

I recognize this month that it is my sole responsibility the creation of my life and destiny. There is no one to blame or hold responsible for the things and situations that I do not create or do not like. I rise in my personal power and become fully responsible of my creation. I rejoice in my power of individuated consciousness.

I breathe in assertiveness, I exhale blame, I breathe in elegance and maturity, I exhale incongruence, I breathe in joy for living, I exhale past misperceptions, I breathe in love, and I exhale joy.

DECEMBER

This month I am committed to see the oneness in all beings, I remember I am at choice every moment that I desire to create myself to be. I choose empowering language, and noble acts and thoughts. Every moment is a new beginning, I keep consistently attuning myself with all universal laws, and I recognize that I am love.

I breathe in love, I exhale Love.

PART IV

The Non-Violent Man
A Self-Agreement on Non-Violence

'LOVE and exclusive possession can never go together.'
Gandhi

Self-agreement on Non-Viloence

After you have studied the sutras and have gotten in to a rhythm of gratitude with the prayers, and have set your mind into a one pointed focus state, through the monthly visualizations, you can embrace and embody the next:

For this section, please proceed to read the agreement, and truly meditate upon opening your mind and heart in to the vastness of a non-violent reality for all human beings and beyond. Visualize the agreement activating each of your cells in to a love field realm, and elevating your consciousness into a higher realm of balance, harmony and inner peace.

Then when you have read each statement carefully and with deep focus, sign and commit to attract the highest peaceful vibratory frequencies into your field from now on.

The Self-agreement on Non-Violence

Today, in this moment, where all that exists is the NOW, I commit to live within the non-violence field of thoughts, actions, words and deeds. I agree with my higher self to work on myself steadfastly and transmute any weaknesses into strengths based on the power of love and the power of kindness that benefits the whole.

I commit to be thankful and live this gratitude every breath of my existence.

I commit and agree to use reason for supporting others not to condemn, judge or prove anything to anyone.

I commit to vibrate in unfathomable faith for humanity's desire for ascension within, its next generations and all its peoples and sentient beings.

I commit to translate into action all my desires for peace and love in the world, creating with this an extended energy field of non-violence and purity of intention that benefits mankind.

I agree with the soul in me, to love myself, and all beings without need of possession. As I love unconditionally I open myself to this gift.

I agree that the non violent field I desire to manifest in the now for myself and all sentient beings will never carry the need to impose suffering on others, instead I focus on self purification and the principle of what I give is what I receive.

I agree that I shall ask nothing in return for giving; with this I am open to the universal goodness.

I agree to remember that the law of love knows no bounds of space or time, and with this, peace is a unipolar experience of the human manifestation as the divine.

I agree to respect life in all of its forms and see all cycles as friends, never as an enemy.'

In my non-violent choice off thinking, talking and living I commit to embrace life as an inspiration and gift for all my fellow human beings to attain self-realization.

I agree that my values and principles will take first priority rank and with these I shall not be disappointed or unmotivated by rocks or obstructions in the way, I shall move forward with leadership, passion and determination.

I shall consistently pray for inward peace and visualize its manifestation out of justice for Earth and its peoples.

I commit to focus on being at peace with myself and with the whole world.

Through meditation and contemplation I shall focus on orderliness, peace, compassion, equanimity, and repose in my daily acts.

I commit to let go of pride and righteousness, to embrace my mistakes as stepping-stones to choose differently the next time, to increase my love, faith and determination towards the goal of unshakable spirit. I walk the path of non-violence with strength and humility, and to see reality as the benevolent manifestation of God Head Realization.

I shall see no tyrant or victim, and recognize these patterns in myself, and work on these to transcend the archetypal energy in to a unified field of peaceful vibration.

I agree and commit to strongly believe in the supreme power of source as consciousness, and respect all different names my human family gives to this power.

I commit and agree to live in truth and, therefore, I let go of any doubts and trust that the present moment and the future of humanity is filled with brilliancy, love and peace, beginning NOW.

_____

Please sign your name here & add the date.

PART V

Rebirthing Masculine Energy in Wholeness and Peace
A Transcendental Rebirthing Visualization

'A man may be born, but in order to be born he must first die, and in order to die he must first awake.' George Gurdjef

Rebirthing Masculine Energy in Wholeness and Peace

After signing the Non-Violence agreement, you are ready for a new birthing of the NEW YOU, a Rebirth of a higher order. For this section, it is suggested that you read it in a quiet place where you wont be disturbed and wear comfortable clothes. As well it is recommended that you have a handheld recorder and record the guided visualization with your own voice and then listen to it, close your eyes and allow yourself to be birthed in newness, wholeness and peace within your masculine energy.

Rebirthing Visualization©43

Visualize yourself inside a Star of David. And imagine this star as a vehicle, as if the star was a car, a vehicle to take you places. Once inside the star, breathe slowly and mindfully through your nose at all times. Feel your heart; touch it with your right hand as you see yourself receiving a golden ray of light inside the star. Then imagine the star, with you inside, going inside the center of this image, known as the Transcendental Rebirthing Sacred Code of AH©44

As this happens, the star begins to move and elevates itself from the three dimensions that we reside, in to the 5th dimension. Here the star, receives another infusion of a violet ray color. As this color infuses your whole being, you begin to say the words "I forgive any analogical moment from my past and ancestral legacies regarding the misuse of masculine power, or misperceptions of what it truly means to embody

---

43   This visualization is copyrighted by The Higher School for Conscious Evolution

44   Sacred Code of AH created and copyrighted by Ivonne Delaflor.

this masculine energy. I let go, forgive and request absolute healing". As this takes place, see the star traveling now towards the 6th, 7th, 8th, 9th, 2nd, 11th and 12th dimension.

Imagine as if you were a child, that the star is growing bigger, and with this you are getting calmer, more peaceful, you are breathing slowly, and you are feeling in your seven chakras the power of masculine energy in a new way. With this happening you say the next words our loud: "I invoke in the higher dimensions of self, the awakening and rebirth of the masculine harmonic energy within me, I take my intent in to the womb of the divine mother, and supported by the divine father, I choose to rebirth my energy field in wholeness, without stories of the past or fears of the future. I ascend in this intent into a realm of possibilities, synergy, action focus and productivity that the male energy brings forth when use wisely. I here and now enter the womb of creation and breathe slowly as it is my turn to embrace the masculine power that is in me".

Now inhale and exhale three times in a more powerful way

And as the third exhalation takes place, imagine the star inside a womb, and begin seeing yourself grow inside the star, think of your highest ideals, dreams and the most positive desires you have for manifestation in your life.

Let go of sorrows, misperceptions or limitations.

Remember in the womb of creation anything is possible, and your intent rebirths as a child would. So if thoughts of doubt or "the ego" show up, just LET IT BE. If the ego is there, or any thought arises that you consider a distraction, just embrace it, allow it to be what is.

And now, repeat the next words out loud three times:

1. "I am safe to embody the masculine energy power, I am, receiving full support from the elementals, and the divine mother supports the divine father for this process. I am the embodiment of balanced male and feminine energy, which rebirths, and heals the masculine energy within me. I am the pure vibration frequency of the divine. I am love, I am source".

2. "I am safe to embody the masculine energy power, I am, receiving full support from the elementals, and the divine mother supports the divine father for this process. I am the embodiment of balanced male and feminine energy, which rebirths, and heals the

masculine energy within me. I am the pure vibration frequency of the divine. I am love, I am source".

3. "I am safe to embody the masculine energy power, I am, receiving full support from the elementals, and the divine mother supports the divine father for this process. I am the embodiment of balanced male and feminine energy, which rebirths, and heals the masculine energy within me. I am the pure vibration frequency of the divine. I am love, I am source".

And as you complete the third repetition, visualize the star coming out of the womb in a shining way. Birthing itself as a light filled with white brilliant light. Now the star and you have become one, and as you see yourself as light you begin to descend back to the 11th, 10th, 9th, 8th, seventh, sixth, fifth, fourth dimension on to the third dimension.

Breathe slowly, inhaling through the nose and exhaling through the mouth. Put your left hand now in your heart, hear your heart beating, put your right hand on top of the left one, and hear your breathing.

And to complete say out loud:

"I am balanced in my energies; both male and female

I am the energy of creation,

I am ever born in the now as the energy of source in congruency,

I am born NOW in wholeness…

I am".

PART VI

Three Invocations to Embody and Receive Support from the Non-Violent Awakened Male Ancestors

"A human being is part of the whole called by us universe, a part limited in time and space. We experience ourselves, our thoughts and feelings as something separate from the rest. A kind of optical delusion of consciousness. This delusion is a kind of prison for us, restricting us to our personal desires and to affection for a few persons nearest to us. Our task must be to free ourselves from the prison by widening our circle of compassion to embrace all living creatures and the whole of nature in its beauty. We shall require a substantially new manner of thinking if mankind is to survive." Albert Einstein

Ancestral Invocations

A spirit of innovation is generally the result of a selfish temper and confined views. People will not look forward to posterity, who never look backward to their ancestors. Edmund Burke

The next invocations are to be used randomly, per your desired need to work in a specific aspect in your life. These invocations are an essential part of this book as they are, in a way the 911 when we perceive a threat, we are in despair, we give in to the illusion of suffering, or our masculine energy, and the masculine energy around us seems out of balance.

It is known that systemic effects that take place within a family system are usually created by hidden legacies of our past, or of our ancestors.

Use this section with grace, gratitude and elegance.

Ancestral invocations are very powerful and should not be taken lightly.

You must have signed the agreement before using these invocations in order to tap into the highest information and protection possible.

Always use this section within the spirit of a win-win scenario for all the beings in your life.

As you practice these invocations, observe subtle shifts in your environment and your loved ones, and mostly in the way you think and perceive things.

INVOCATION I
Ancestral Mind

"It is one of the goals of religions to liberate mankind as far as possible from the bondage of egocentric cravings, desires, and ancestral fears –Albert Einstein

Beloved ancestors, both from father and mother lineages, you have walked in time before me, in a field of love, choices and possibilities, I invoke the wisdom in you to set in order that which appears out of balance. Take back what is yours, and set free the mind of your future generations beginning with me. Let us carry what is ours in grace and humility.

I invoke benevolence and grace and request your support. I invoke divine alignment, serenity, and mind healing.

I invoke forgiveness where necessary, and set the deck clear for the present moment to walk forward in steady determination, consistency, sense of purpose, and awakened mission.

I invoke freedom of mind, and am embodying higher frequencies of thought field vibratory manifestation now.

I invoke these all with love, and am grateful as I recognize it is granted, NOW.

INVOCATION II
Ancestral Body

"All religions, arts and sciences are ancestral branches of the same tree. All these ancestral aspirations are directed toward ennobling man's life, lifting it from the sphere of mere physical existence and leading the individual towards freedom." Unknown

I command and invoke, with firm clarity and purpose, that all ancestral loyalties based on blind love and fragmented uncompleted life situations are relinquished from my field now. I release these hidden legacies and send them back to the source where they came from. I release all physical inherited ailments from my psyche and physical form and release with this my next generations from the consequence of fate.

The reality is that only bodies die, yet the human spirit is irrevocably immortal. With this I send gratitude to my ancestors and release my field from any illness inheritance in body, mind, and spirit.

Only I can live in the body gifted to me by source. My cellular memory expands in newness and restores in to its original blueprint essence, free of entanglements, and free of that which does not belongs to me.

I send waves of light to what was, yet what is, is the source of my focus, as my path is filled with the Now, and I invoke the acceptance of the full realization that my past does not determines my future.

It is invoked and received this as granted, now.

INVOCATION III
Ancestral Spirit

"Our greatest responsibility is to be good ancestors" Jonas Salk

I invoke the blessings of my higher conscious ancestors to activate and bless the circle of life and compassion that I create with my family members. Please bless us with consciousness and awareness, free us from old ancient debts that are not ours, walk with us as benevolent spirits that protect, support, and witness the evolution of love in peace, grace, and ecstatic life manifestation.

Honor us by allowing our tribute to you to be received with the acts and presence we manifest in our current reality and experience.

Gift us with loving wisdom, and respect the passage of time and space.

We are now the new ancestors of our future generations, and with this we invoke the ancient spirit of humanity to rise in consciousness, to rise in freedom, to rise in nobility, and mostly love.

I am the spirit of humanity, and I receive what is mine to receive, and bless with this the future generations by respecting their individuated source consciousness.

PART VII

The Heart-felt Sharings

I will never forget the two of us watching the Sox win the series together. It is one of many favorite memories I have of you and I together. Not a day goes by where I am not thankful that you are here with us experiencing these special events and family additions. Who knows, there may even be a Chicago Stanley Cup Parade in your future. :) I love you Dad! Matt Moorman

The Heart-felt Sharings

The next section is the compilation of the contribution from different fellow human beings, who shared their own perceptions, and personal experiences in relationship with the Divine Father. This book would not be complete without the real life experience of our human family members regarding the masculine energy and their own father experiences.

After each of their sharing, I offer a humble commentary that is related to the Sutras and principles of this book.

I am eternally grateful for their contribution[45].

At the end of this section you will have the opportunity, if you choose, to write your own heart felt sharing for the Divine Father energy.

Now just read, enjoy, and connect with other members of our human family within the field of The Divine Fathers' love. As together we remember that We all are ONE.

---

45 The contributions here shared by different individuals, are fully authorized to be published in this book, each sharing is copyrighted by its own author, and Divine Father & Ivonne Delaflor have received their permission to post their sharing in this book, and comment with you all. Some of the names or last names have been avoided or changed for privacy matters, yet most of the authors have shared their real names.

The Sunday Paper

By Chick Moorman

I remember the Sunday paper. Not all of it. Just a certain section and a Sunday morning ritual at our home in Chicago.

It must have been 1940 something. I'm guessing 1947. That would make me five years old. My brother was two years younger.

Each Sunday morning my brother and I would race to the front door to see if the paper had been delivered. We wanted to be the one to bring it in and get it ready for the ritual.

There was no TV to turn on. Handheld family disconnect machines had not been invented yet. So we focused on the paper, mostly the comic section.

The comic section was removed from the paper and taken to its usual place of honor, the middle of the living room floor. There, it would sit until our father finished his morning coffee. Anticipation increased as our patience and the coffee in his cup slowly dwindled.

When the coffee drinking subsided, the ritual began. My father position himself on the floor. My brother and I took our usual positions with me on the left and my brother to my dad's right. That's the way we configured ourselves, laying on the floor with the paper spread out in front of us, every Sunday morning as my father read the comics to us.

Looking back on this ritual sixty-four years later, I realize this is my earliest memory of an experience with literacy. It is my first recollection of being read to. It is the first time that I know of that I wanted to know what the words said. I wished I could read, like my dad.

The content of the comics are gone now. I don't remember anything about what the characters did or said. I have only vague recollections of the specific comics. I recall Dick Tracy (the detective), Dagwood, and that's about it.

That the words and the themes are long gone from my memory is of no consequence. Vastly more important are the images and feelings that remain etched in my consciousness.

I remember a young father and two young boys lying on the floor together. I don't remember my father's words, but I remember the excitement in his voice as he helped bring the characters to life. I remember what he felt like as my brother and I laid next to him straining to get closer to the pictures and to him. I can tell you what he smelled like, what he looked like, and how it felt to be read to every Sunday morning. It felt good.

Thanks Dad.

COMMENTARY:

The memories of childhood are priceless nuggets of learning, mastery, and love. What we do matters, only 100% of the time, we never know how our words, our habits, our rituals will impact the life of someone we love, we meet, we encounter. The father in this sharing, surely knew where his place was to be, a Father, offering his children a moment of absolute presence, where they become the receivers of his attention, love and teachings. Spoken or unspoken, the teacher is always present; and with his actions he models, ignites and enlightens the minds and hearts of those around him, specially his children.

Everyone in our life is a teacher, and little did this father know, that the young Boy, who has grateful memories of this Sunday habit, will become not only a lover of the words he wished he could have read from that Sunday paper, but who grew up as a conscious adult that has empowered thousands of individuals through teaching them skills to use their spoken words and language to increase responsibility. This boy, now a man and teacher, has taught thousands of Parents to change the use of their words in order to use them to uplift, support, and empower all children. Yes, this father was surely a teacher, and with his modeling and personal choices , his son became a teacher himself.

Gratitude for the simple moments in life is the true ticket to eternal abundance, and this heart felt sharing is sure filled with this energy. It may be time to grab a Sunday paper, and say thanks to the teacher called life.

My Father was Always There

By Alex Slucki

The day after I began reading Part 1 of the Divine Father Book, I finally attended my first Hatha Yoga class in Terrassa... as it turns out, the instructor (and owner of the school) is named Ruben, that is MY FATHER's name, and a very unusual name here in Cataluña, where most people you'll meet are named Jordi, Manel, Francesc... but not Ruben (actually it is 'Reuben'. In Hebrew it might translate as: Reu: 'look at' Ben: 'the son'.

Isn't that a beautiful metaphor? My father left this world when I was twelve, and back then, I felt like two fathers had actually abandoned me. I lost my faith and became quite skeptical for over a decade. There was no Male Divine to follow, I felt like I had to follow my own heart and protect my own self from the world. The Divine Mother was very busy trying to find her own balance.

As it turns out, this is probably the BEST gift both my Fathers could offer me. For Male energy experiences an initiation into maturity and it involves being able to see one's Self as One Is, without help... which doesn't imply lack of supervision.

The Fathers were always there. The physical one had become an ancestor, watching me from a place of acceptance of my journey; offering me the freedom to choose my own way and make my own decisions. While Divine Father had gently allowed me to rediscover him in the fullness of his grace, with his many faces and voices. Ruben the yoga Teacher had indeed become the Father. His voice was gentle, pure, embracing, yet powerful, focused and poetic. No one reads living poetry like the Father. And I believe his best poem is the sensuousness he lets us discover in the Mother. A perfect, divine arrangement. My faith is fully restored.

Blessings and love,
Alex Slucki,
Aka, Swami Ramananda

COMMENTARY:

To experience the death of a father or mother at a young age is quite an intense experience. In his wrritings, Alex shares with us the abandonment feelings this caused to him, not only from his Physical Father, but from God, as the Divime Energy that he felt within his father, also had abandoned him.

Over the years, with his personal path and choices, he found not only beautiful metaphors in why this event in his life had not occurred against him but in his favor. He redefined the meaning he gave to this experience, he gave a place to his Father as a gracious ancestor, a protector of his path, and he opened up to receive more love of the Divine Father energy that is ever present, and speaks to us through everything, and everyone, every single moment.

He indeed found true poetry in his experience, where Father and Son become One.

Grief transformed, is pure uncinditional Love; which is the gateway to the restoration of faith in our power and human spirit.

The True Father is much like a True Mother
By Swami Nadiananda

As I read the "invitation" to share experiences of love toward the father figure, my mind took a turn in another direction (hmmmm...well, I guess THAT'S not unusual!)

As it turns out, the timing was divine...as usual! If you desire to read further, my thoughts were as follows....

The True Father....

Once, during a communication with my spirtual taecher, Babaji, I remarked, "Worry is just an excuse to control." I was referring to my own father, who spent much of my and my brother's lives expressing worry/fear about our safety, our futures...and later about our children's safety, our children's futures. Yes, my father often exhibited the tyrant persona...BUT..no matter the intensity of this, somehow.WE ALWAYS FELT LOVED!

So....what are the characteristics of the True Father....one who demonstrates all-ways love for his kids?

The True Father, when he assumes the role of parent, whether biological or by assertion, makes a commitment for eternity.

The True Father encourages his kids to strive to reach their highest human potential, all the while recognizing their divinity.

The True Father remains steadfastly at his kids' sides, always walking beside them with a quick hand to catch the falls and comfort the hurts he knows are only temporary.

The True Father, even when thinking, "Father Knows Best," allows his kids to follow their own paths...but he is always present to offer support. The word abandonment is not in his vocabulary.

The True Father recognizes that his kids may require reassurance of his love and fidelity, and he gives it with sweet tenderness as consistently as the sun rises.

The True Father is much like a True Mother...

Love and Blessings,
Swami Nadiananda
Co Founder of the Maitri Order
www.maitriorder.org

COMMENTARY:

The way we parent is mostly based in how we were parent, this happens until we raise our consciousness and decide to bring those teachings to a new level of life and awareness. In this sharing we see that no matter what was happened in the children's life, projected by the fear or ignorance of the Father, there was a little girl who chose to love him no matter what. Children will always be the greatest teachers of love, they will create a hero out of a dragon, and they will create a path where there is a wall. Here the child chose love and respect, and loyalty to the father, and chose to grow in to a human being that knows what a Father that loves his children really does from a space of wisdom. Father or Mother, concepts and labels of the energies of creation, are both one energy guardianship of the spirits of the future generations, ever teaching, ever nurturing, and ever presenting the gifts of self-realization to the children. Such Grace is the experience of being human.

What a Father Represents for Me
By Claudia Molina, Swami Ananda.

When I think about the word father…what comes to me is the presence of God, The One, as his male self and also of my spiritual guide, friend and master: Babaji.

There are several qualities and attributes I envision when I think about this

Protection is the first quality that comes to my mind and heart. My divine father is always present for me to guard over me. I feel secure and safe just to know of his existence. I have the certainty I can count on him, whatever the circumstances and situations are, and that he will listen to me, honor me, respect me, acknowledge me and provide his loving advice, without any agenda, without controlling, without imposing, out of unconditional love.

Another attribute is strength imbued with loving care. For me he is like the element fire, full of magnificent and powerful energy that ignites action, intent, and a creative force. Is the willingness behind the intent to see it come forth. It is ever expanding energy.

Determination is another quality I see in him. He knows with certainty where he is going and what he desires to accomplish, manifest. There is no hesitation or doubt, but a strong confidence in himself, his worth, his talents and in how to direct them to honor himself and serve others on his way.

He is firm and compassionate at the same time. His firmness is filled with love and appreciation for others. He treats people with kindness and respect. You can see his sweet and melting heart and at the same time recognize his very strong foundation. And when I see this, I see a modeling of perfect balance.

He has a sense of humor and likes to play jokes. His sense of responsibility perfectly matches his love for play. He knows how to have fun and enjoy himself in the company of others. His sense of humor just makes me laugh all the time and rejoices my heart. I love that he has this sense of humor and does not take everything so seriously and that he reminds me of this all the time, through his loving words or his own modeling.

I feel so happy, fortunate for him to be part of my life. What he is for me is precisely the Father Figure, attributes, qualities, and values that a child could ever look forward and follow as a loving modeling of what a father is, as the male self that is also contained within myself.

Claudia
Author of ; *TANTRA, The art of Sacred Sexuality as a Gateway to Ascension*

COMMENTARY:

The Dream of all children is to have a "perfect" Father, a Father that never makes mistakes, that is always present, that is always giving and loving…a father, that is practically not granted the right of make any mistakes…or be human.

Our Fathers, mothers, are beings that learn the path of being Mom and Dad as they walk through life.

Sometimes the qualities we cant find in our own father, yet we desired him to have, and we cant find in there, are the qualities that due to this apparent lack, we foster and grow within from the depths of our soul.

We sometimes find the father figure that we need, in others masculine energy representatives such as in the male energy of the sun, or of a spiritual teacher, an awaken warrior, all delivering the energies of safety, protection, and stability. Yet if we see closely with our hearts, we will find, however cathartic or convoluted our experience is or was with our biological father, these qualities in him. We will find the presence of source. The teacher, the student, all as a mirror of our own divinity, of our own strength, of our own teacher within. We then open our minds to love, to forgiveness and with this we awaken the father within, and we begin to give our inner child the exact things we expected our Mother and Father to give to us, and what a joyous day that is, where my expectations, or visions of the prefect Father disappear, and I finally become ONE with him.

The Hand of the Father: Understanding
By Kristi Nimmo

What does father represent to me? I think of my father, Dad, and the pleasant recognition that if I have a father, then I am also a daughter. This is an instant identity, a characteristic that is a gift to cherish and grow. Here is an opportunity to love! I think of my most recent visit home, my father and I, side by side, holding hands, in a place of worship. If that is not a mirror of the cosmos, I do not know what is.

The hand of the father, I once sent Dad a tracing of my hand. He was recovering from a serious illness. I wrote a note that said for him to press the tracing to his heart and know my love. When we met again, face to face, we pressed hands to hearts and we said, "I love you," and in turn answered, "I know."

Kristi Nimmo
www.astonespeaks.com

COMMENTARY:

When we van meet our Father with the grace of presence, the stories, the identities disappear. The grace of it, the gloriousness of the moment, unites us closer with our loved ones that no other thought, emotion, or thing can do. The identities are dropped; love allows itself to be, to be breathed, and to become a form that we call Father or Daughter. We get to experience he unity on diversity and we get to journey the adventure of identifying with a role of son, daughter, and create an outside reflection of ourselves as a father, mother, God/

There are no words to describe this love, for love is the reverberation of the truth, which is never lost, is never gained, it always is…TRUTH.

I Am a Divine Father
By Swami Arjunananda

When I think of the Father energy I think of three things:

1) My father
2) The Divine Masculine energy of God/Source
3) And myself as the father of my own inner child and my future now children

My father through his modeling ways taught me how to be a gentleman, to be respectful of others, to keep my word and do the best I could in everything I did. My father taught me to be committed and responsible in little things like always making sure I attended my basketball games/practices. I admire his dedication to provide a quality life for all my family and his unique ways of showing affection like a warm touch with his entire palm on top of my shoulder as he smiles.

The masculine aspect of God/Source for me represents that energy that listens to and answers my questions, the energy of motion, protection, support and manifestation. This is the energy that is at the service of the Divine Mother and inspires me to be part of the Great Work.

And as the father of my own inner child I perceive this inner energy as a loving parent that is very willing to play with his child, take care of him, protect him and teach him in the best of his ways how to live a life of inner and outer abundance with the deepest sense of gratitude and willingness to share this with the ones he loves. And I also see myself as a future-now parent giving one of the greatest gifts I can ever possibly give to my future-now children by constantly working on myself…the gift of a clean slate and no entanglements so that they can walk their unique paths and fulfill their own purposes here on Earth.

I AM a Divine Father,

Gustavo Castañer
Swami Arjunananda
AuricCalibration.com

COMMENTARY:

The Father, the Son, and Spirit, three apparent forms of the same source consciousness. The aspect of this trinity is the manifestation of oneness. To honor all aspects of reality as one, to join them and gather them in the temple of our hearts, and vibrate with great love the rituals of acceptance for what is, is to honor oneself, is to embark in a journey of Omni-love this very moment. This is the place where we grow in strength, character, and embodiment of the higher values that support our human family to strive, our children to be free, our women to be safe, and our own inner master to be born again and again for the sake of experiencing a higher vision of love for the Father, the child and the spirit, (seen as God, or as source consciousness) where gratitude can truly flow from our hearts and minds for the experience of being…simply being.

Father, Father, Father[46]
By Drew LaHaye

Father, father, father,
You never let me down
These cold eyes can sleep at night knowing' you're around
Father, father, father
You taught me right from wrong
You have kept me from singing' that same old song
(And now I'm on my way)
(I'll never look back one damn day)
Oh but I'm lost and so alone
Please bring me back home
And leave me there to stay
(oh no no no no no)
(Oh no no no no no)

Father father father
What do I do now?
I'm lost and just don't know how,
To make it all go away, make it all go away
Please tell me today

(solo)

(Now son you know what to do)
(don't let these fears and worries bother you)
Gotta keep movin on

---

46   ©By Andrew (Drew) LaHaye, song first recorded in June 2009

Gotta keep goin strong now
(OH no no no no no)
(Oh no no no no no)

Father father father
I am a new man
These tired eyes can sleep at night with your wisdom in hand
(now I know you taught me well)
(These feelings and fears I will not dwell)
Gotta keep movin on
(Oh no no no no no)
OH no no no no no)

COMMENTARY:

This sharing, this sacred song, is a true example of the importance of a Father-Son relationship. The embrace, the support, and most of all what matters most; THE PRESENCE.

The greatest gift we can give one another is this; pure presence, being fully HERE.

When moments of despair, or sorrow manifest in life, we can go deep within to the voice of the Father, call for him…ad if we do, we will hear, through our inner voice, his heart letting us know: "it's all going to be O.K., it's all O.K., I am with you".

In the presence of a Father a boy strives, a girl feels safe, a woman loves, and a Mother births…such a gift, such a miracle, and such a song of love.

Divine Sympathy
By Hanna Taleb

I wrote down ten days ago, two pages about my father, about how I saw him and what he represented to me. Since then, I noticed that my relation with my father has been evolving and that I've been growing in my relation with my father as well as in my relation with myself. Those have been ten interesting days during which I experienced physical unease along with emotional unease till I integrated the new realizations I had about myself, the beliefs I held concerning my father etc.

I feel it is no coincidence if I'm currently staying with my parents in the apartment where I was born, waiting to deliver my baby very soon. It is no coincidence either if I read two weeks ago a small sentence, which I reacted to and which was talking about "maternology" and the psychology of the expecting mother. The article said that "maternology" was closely linked to the relation of the expecting mom with her own father. I had a sort of reaction while reading that: "With my father? What does the father have to do with that? It's surely about women and mothers only!"

I've realized since then that I wasn't totally at peace in my relation with my father and that I was even unconsciously denying my father's active role in conceiving me!

I also realized that I had been feeling an emotional distance with my father and sadness for not being able to be closer to him.

After writing down about my father, and having a difficult week of physical and emotional upheaval I finally woke up with a different mindset and realized that I had matured and gained in consciousness. I was feeling much more serene and calm, with myself, with my father and with all.

I feel today that I've gained sympathy towards my father and I'm looking at him with more affection and love instead of looking at him with judgment and criticism. I am also now at ease whenever he expresses his emotions instead of feeling that a father doesn't have the right to do so, that he's supposed to stick to his role as a tough teacher or "the representative at home of rules and regulations".

Now I feel him closer to me. I feel also myself more feminine and gentle.

I've opened more my heart to him but also to myself and I've integrated within me a "Father figure" that is closer to me, that is kinder and more loving. This has been a true gift!

Having shared this experience of the last two weeks I will share what my father has represented to me for long and what he still represents to me in the Now:

My father has always represented to me the notions of order, laws, organization and the mental and rational aspect of life. I've always seen him as the perfect student, the serious one, the person who's always seeking what is "right" to do.

He used to appear to me to be very strict and rigid, sometimes also too critical and judgmental of others. I used to feel respect, fear and admiration towards my father.

For a long time I used to fear being criticized or judged as harshly as my father would do towards other people. I am grateful for the lessons I learnt from my father and glad to be done with that fear.

My father is a physicist and a mathematician but also a successful engineer who was one of the first founders of the first consulting engineering firm in the Middle East. He is what we call a "self made-man". I used to feel very impressed with his intellectual faculties, his strong personality and his path of life. He is a sort of public figure in Lebanon and being considered as "his daughter" was for long my identity. I've developed a sort of intellectual complex that all my outer successes at school/university…couldn't erase. I used to feel that my father made it hard for me to feel proud of myself. I used to feel that I would never gain his esteem or anyone else's esteem unless I proved myself to be Albert Einstein Junior! Of course this had been all my own work, setting the bar too high, judging harshly myself, being rude towards myself, seeking intellectual perfection. Now I see things very differently and I am grateful for the lessons learnt and I know that the only esteem I look for is my own and that I've been putting those challenges myself and that my true mission, the one that I feared for long not being able to fulfill is my soul's mission and that as long as I am working on clearing all the limiting beliefs I may have and focusing on that mission my internal father will be happy.

Another important aspect in my father that I still see in the Now is his confidence and faith. I see him as a solid soul that doesn't get too much involved in the ups and downs of life.

He is wise, serene, and very patient and doesn't drown himself into emotional "dramas". He represents to me calmness, support and protection at all levels.

As a kid I would seek for my father's presence or advice whenever I would feel my emotions were taking over and would look for his point of view that was always wise and emotionally detached.

I am grateful I learnt confidence and faith in life mainly thanks to my father.

Finally I would say that in those two weeks my relation with myself, my inner father through also the physical presence of my father, has become much clearer. I've clearly realized that all that I used to see or still see in my father are reflections of my beliefs about myself. The challenges I thought my physical father was presenting to me were challenges my inner father was facing.

I can say today that the male energy in me has been taking more and more its place to balance the feminine energy in me. I feel that both the male and female energy have got more into balance.

Today I looked at my father, smiled at him and questioned myself "what do you still see in him"? I realized that I don't see him as the severe judge anymore, nor as a person without emotions all those beliefs have been cleared.

He smiled back and I was happy. I realized though that I still see him as a serious, uptight person who doesn't laugh enough in life and in whose presence I find it difficult to laugh and have fun. But I know that as soon as I realize something, a shift in my consciousness starts.

So Now I'm looking at my father and I can sense that I am smiling, that the child in me is finally ready to go out from the shadow of the father, to relax, play and laugh as long as she wants to.

COMMENTARY:

To embrace the masculine and the feminine with equanimity is true liberation. When we negate one part of creation, we are, unconsciously negating the other. Both male/female, Father /Mother are necessary for the balance of life. Our projections, and inner imbalances sometimes take flight in making it seem that its coming from outside forces, either our fathers didn't do it right , or our Mothers didn't nurture us "appropriately". To honor the Father, is to Honor the Mother, and to honor both as one is the beginning to honor oneself; and with this we cease all fragmentation, we become the experience of totality, and give birth to wholeness.

Play
By Swami Bhalananda

My father is 82 years old and still healthy. He likes watching TV, eating good foods that my mother cooks, gardening in summer and clearing snow in winter. I just visited my parents who live in Sapporo, Japan one month ago. I felt in this trip that my perception to my father has been different after the works of several TRs[47] and clearing my imprints. I am able to feel that I am just their daughter and to receive their love. I don't feel that they need my help anymore. They are all right and no problem. I am impressed at what my parents passed through and accomplished in their life. I didn't feel it before.

I recall that I played with my father a lot when I was a kid. Since my sister was born, I think I was closer to him. I remember his warm foot in a cold winter night before I fell asleep. I know he loved me a lot. He always allows me to do most of things I want to. I am really grateful to his tolerance and trust to me. Of course, we had some difficult times, though.

I feel emotional while I am writing this essay because new awareness is showing up inside of me. My family lived in the countryside of northern Japan, where have a huge amount of snow and temperature drops below -20C in winter. We lived in a small house. My memory is that the house was covered with beautiful white snow but the inside was warm. I realized that I never had any doubt that we were frozen. I am touched by what we were given by my father without saying.

For me, father represents quiet, security, love and trust.
I am really happy that he is still healthy in his 80th.

Toshie Yoneyama, Japan.
Swami Bhalananda
http://www.butterflydreamusa.webs.com/

---

47 www.transcendentalrebirthing.com

COMMENTARY:

This sharing shows us that the warmth of home is created not only by Mother but by the Father presence as well, and invites us to realize the gifts that the father gives to us, sometimes so silently that we could forget his presence is there. The struggles, the joys, all come part as the holistic experience of being human, and the blessing and gift to experience the presence of a father.

Divine Father Deepened My Awareness

By Swami Shirananda

I choose to dedicate this to my biological father, FJR.

Sitting in my car at a stop sign on my 34th birthday, I saw a man across the street that looked exactly like my father. His radiating smile of love's essence was flowing my way. Telepathically he was saying…'I love you in all ways, always.'

WOW, I was stunned for the entire day!!!!! I had not seen my father's image since he passed away when I was seven.

Years later, while driving on the freeway just outside of town, I suddenly felt my Father's presence in the passenger seat of my car. The divine energy was unmistakably my Father signaling his unconditional love. I immediately pulled over to the shoulder on the freeway to give space to this unexpected visit.

The gifts of these two experiences bridged my adult ordinary world to the multi- dimensions I lived as a child.

Soon after this second experience, I apprenticed in the Navajo tradition and became passionate about my relationship with Father Sky and Mother Earth. I felt the lack of parental bonding and somehow, it just felt right to have these eternal parents who were providing for humanity in a very functional way. They were always ready to listen and give me guidance when I choose to connect with them. Many times their signs were given to me in nature, through their other children in the plant, animal and mineral kingdoms or in the elemental world of earth, water, fire and air. And sometimes through my sense in smell, light, sound or vibration from within my body, they would signal to me even their desire to communicate with me. Once we reconnected in these realms, I began to process what I perceived as losses.

Frequently in the Native American tradition, I would reach through these dimensions outside ordinary time, the realms that most adults seem to have forgotten.

My Dad's visitations provided me a missing experience that had not occurred during my childhood....an available Father. This was a deep transcendental healing experience. He had not forgotten he and me shared his remorse for not knowing how to be there for me.

Surges of total delight flowed through his visitations. Although there were only a few of these experiences, they changed my attitude in 'What is a Father'? These 'divine' appearances, somehow allowed me to drop my expectations for what a Father should be like!!!!!! They began a healing for me and later, how I perceive other children's fathers.

Through time, these non-ordinary experiences influenced my professional life. My focus in service includes children and their parents. Frequently, the children's fathers find reasons why they can't be there more for their children. Rather than have an unsupportive attitude, I choose to follow the parent's ability to participate and continue to offer opportunities for each to recreate with their child.

Now I ask the question ' **how can this father align harmonically with his son/daughter?**' This shift in my perspective is ever widening for new possibilities for families to grow and support each other in playful activities together.

I give thanks to you, Dad for sharing a transcendence experience.

I am grateful for the times you visited me from beyond this realm.

My remembrance of you models for me the power of humbleness and truth. I continue to grow and learn how there is more for me to surrender to in life. Your visitations support my walk in my personal and fun service I bring to humanity. I love you.

Thank you for my life, dearest Father...you are truly divine.

Your loving daughter,
Serena D. Rees Sutherland
(Swami Shirananda)
www.youcancountonchange.com

COMMENTARY:

The importance of Father is evident for any child who wishes to soar. Here, Serena shares with us how a missing experience was fulfilled by receiving a higher vision of love and visitations by his father in the visual world.

How important truly the fathers' presence is for what we are to create as adults and share with the next generations.

Thanks to a change in attitude, to the desire, like Serena, to see the gift within the experience, Serena now supports and have supported thousands of families and children to thrive and receive the state of presence required by all children to be who they are. She also welcomed her father back in to her awareness, and with this healed any misperceptions or past wounds that may have occurred.

Father energy is extremely healing, and when we welcome it with no judgment and forgiveness we are giving a gift to ourselves, of presence, safety and love.

The Father Energy
By Swami Bhimananda

Heavenly Father, the God within, the Spirit,
Babaji, Abba, Vader, Père, Padre
Guardian and Protector of the Soul
Modeling his children life through
Self-responsible acting and playful reacting
Supporting the female energy
Of nurturing and compassion
By adding his guidance, action and protection
Now go in silence and visualize
One joyful experience you shared as a child
With your human father and realize
That this one moment of light entering your mind
Of maybe watching a soccer game together
Anchors a sacred vibration
Of love in your heart
An instant healing comes into manifestation
The male and female energy merges
Creating a perfect inner synergy
Of absolute harmony and unity
Thank you Father

Sylvia Dokter
Aka Swami Bhimananda
www.rebirthinginjoy.com

COMMENTARY:

Father and mother together truly birth the ultimate embodiment of their love through a child and through the experience of unity on diversity. The eternal dance of polarities keeps the balance of the all that is. The safety the father provides, the nurturing the mother conveys, and the joy that the child transpires are but one and the same as the poetry writes itself from the heart of God, where Father, Mother and Child are ONE.

How to Be a Father
By Swami Amarananda

Dear Dad,

If I can single out one most important quality, it is this:

You taught me how to be a father.

In your own way, you chose and were guided, perhaps by my inner child, to teach through example. It is a way I have chosen to do and not to do. There are ways I choose differently with my own magnificent son. Yet, as the headstrong, rebellious child I can choose to be, perhaps your methods were what I best understood. By example, we teach. And, I must say, I can still embody the headstrong nature, the rebelliousness that can also be known as a passion for sovereignty. J

The other beautiful thing you brought to me ...and all of the rest of the family ...was, and is, that great sense of humor. It was clearly a part of your young life growing up, as we all noticed the same, subtle and outrageous sense of humor that pervaded the gatherings of your siblings. Then, I know I noticed the origins of this sense of humor in your father, a man shell-shocked by the challenges of living the 3D experience. Yet, the wry quip was always there. The unexpected, often ironic twist that brought the laughter up from the diaphragm to ring out in the family atmosphere.

You are loved more with each passing day. Dad, this is my written tribute to you and to the laughing legacy which will forever grace the lives of those close to you. I love you, Dad.

Your Grateful Son,
Blessings and Love Always,
Phil/Amar
Founder of The Maitri Order
www.maitriorder.org

P.S: I am thinking, too, that one day, when we meet again, we can do a little fishing together. What do you think? And, perhaps I will once again sing for you on top of your favorite Japanese chow table. Hmmm … It will be lots of fun

COMMENTARY:

The power of legacy is as strong as all the oceans in our planet, it can be quiet, it can rise, it can nurture, protect and give life…legacies of joy, of modeling attitudes, values, ethics, and perhaps even gifting us sometimes with what seems to be a lack, only to find the strength within ourselves to make things happen. Oh what joy the legacies, and what an important part of this gift is to give tribute for the father generosity of living, learning and gifting us with such opportunities of learning and loving.

Container of Safety
By Swami Bharatananda

Where is our first opportunity to know the energy of the Divine Father? Usually it is through our relationship with our own genetic father or father figure.

As I began to write of my father, I found the memories all mixed together. What I remembered and loved, and all mixed into those memories was the awareness of my child self-longing for more: more of his time, more of his attention. Physically strong, athletic, confident, handsome with black wavy hair, blue eyes and a ready smile. He worked long hours 6.5 days per week, and as a small child I remember being so excited when he would come home, coming in the back door, taking off his oil stained clothing and putting on clean clothes and washing his hands and face. It was as if the sun would shine inside the house, bringing warmth and light when he came home.

For me my father created a container of safety. I could and did ask my father most anything, and share with him many feelings. Two of my most favorite times growing up were dinners at the kitchen table where we would talk about everything, lingering long after the meal was done and the rare occasions where he would take me with him on Sundays, when he only worked 4 hours instead of 10. I would ride with him up to check on oil wells. I followed him into oil leases, climbed among tank farms, went into derricks and we would talk and laugh. For those special times, it was as if he opened a door and let me into his world away from home.

My father was a man with a ready smile, who conveyed a genuine liking of and interest in others. He seemed equally admired by men, women and children. In reviewing my experiences as his daughter, I pay tribute to how much he shaped my view of men, men's relationships with women, and what is their role with children. My father was not authoritative in the sense of bossy, abusive or controlling. Rather he influenced by his presence, his story telling, his ability to laugh at himself, his "code" about being a man and his modeling of how to live and be. He became, in the mind and heart of my child self, someone who was larger that life itself. From the child perspective, he supported my mother 100%. No matter what went on between them, to me they were a team. Always working together, supporting each other and granting to each other respect, appreciation and tribute and creating consistency between them with me.

I also came to appreciate in my adult years how unresolved issues between the mother and father, can, even if not shared in words, affect the sense of harmony in the home and the sense of well being of the child. Both in the lives of my parents, my life and in the life of my daughter, I have seen the power of the divine father energy manifest and carry forward to affect the lives of the children and grandchildren. Sometimes ancestral issues dim its brilliance, by free will choices not in alignment with the Divine Father blueprint. Transcendental Rebirthing has given me great appreciation and increased understanding for how the blind love of children can carry forward into adult life the unfinished business of ancestors.

I am in gratitude for this opportunity to give tribute: to the Divine Father energy, which is held within each of us, and to my father for his laughter, enjoyment of life, finding his passion, responsibility for family, modeling and the sense of safety and protection that he gifted to me and to our home. I am in gratitude and appreciation for all of who he was.

Linda Heller
(Swami Bharatananda)
www.beyourbrilliancenow.com

Commentary:

If you want to find the good things in life, you will do it regardless of the past experiences. Determination will bring this gift into your life.

Here we can see how the vision of Linda's Father also supported her in her view and respect of the male energy. She also found the energy of the father within and the courage to heal what she called unresolved issues in order to move forward and embrace the father energy and set herself free. Such joy to find out that we can have a great relationship with our parents, when we realize that they did the best they could, they taught us exactly what we needed to learn, and they showed us with their own unique character, words and ways, that they loved us… and in return, we find the unconditional love we always have had for them.

My Father

By Swami Pracuryananda

As I started thinking of my father, my thoughts went to the two young fathers in my family, my nephew and nephew-in-law. Their children are 5 months and 7 months old. I was privileged to observe these two young men support their wives during the pregnancies, the birth, and now the care of the children and the over whelming joy and love they demonstrate. Watching them, I felt at peace. The peace came from seeing them in the future exhibiting this support, joy, and love through open clear communication with their children as they have exhibited with the mothers' of the children.

Looking back at my father through the filter of memories, I knew he was there in supportive and loving way but not expressed in words. He was always there at dinnertime and he shared the cooking, especially his specialties. On Sundays we usually had a family drive or something together as a family. He went to work and mom was with us, working on philanthropic projects, with friends and family. From my perspective he was always there for us kids and mom but more in the background, not very talkative but there.

I also saw times when my mom supported dad in different ways. One major time was when she went to work in his business. After mom died, I became aware of other more subtle ways she supported him.

As I am writing this and looking at my father and my relation I see the need for and importance of communication. This I say from the perspective of the daughter in a father daughter relationship. There is so much that I desire to speak to him about now and I see in the past where rough times could have been smoother and the good times could have been brilliant.

Grace Brandt
Swami Pracuryananda

Commentary:

The importance of open and loving communication is essential for the growth and nurturing of any relationship. All children crave this with their fathers, and they look for it in any possible way they can. This sharing is a good reminder for all the Male energy on how thirsty the child is for his fathers' soothing words, for his loving listening and his warmth embrace. Yes, a father that embraces these qualities, he is not only vulnerable to feel but also becomes extremely powerful. With this power children awaken, they get inspired, they soar, and as Grace shares here, they manifest a brilliant outcome, a brilliant future, by the fuel of the Fathers Love.

Because I thought he knew
By Swami Alishananda

My relationship with my father was one of deep love, reverence, admiration, *and* fear. My "Daddy" and I were close. I would ask him anything *because I thought he knew*. I have fond memories of our special time together. He took me fishing, taught me about bugs, trees, leaves, and had a deep appreciation for the intricacies of nature – only now do I appreciate this. I was one of seven children and the next to the youngest.

My father also had a deep anger, which would appear from time to time. From this, I developed a fear of his anger and fearing whatever triggered the anger. I feared him coming home from work yelling. I didn't know it at the time, but I held resentment towards him for this. I felt ambivalence towards him and ambivalence, guilt, towards my feelings. I kept a somewhat safe distance from him so as not to get hurt. I articulated these feelings and found a sense of peace through counseling in adulthood.

I saw him as this great figure especially at work: smart and intelligent, savvy, big in stature. He focused on being strong in his presence, at 6' 3" this could be intimidating, He a sharp tongue and yet a kindness to him. (This is something I feel all of us developed - a criticalness towards ourselves and others.)

My memories of my father include watering the flowers, the tomatoes and planting, - he loved plants of all kinds, and he loved to observe Earth. As he grew older and retired, he grew softer and gentler. He was now planting flowers in *my* yards.

My relationship with him carried out in my relationship with other males. I was mostly terrified of being my real self around other males. I did not allow myself to get really close emotionally until after I turned 30 and met my husband.

While working on this assignment, I had a dream regarding particular activities of mine in high school. I was reminded of *my* responsibility in my relationship with my father. While he commanded respect from others, I went through a period of not respecting him or myself, while doing teenager related activities, which I later regretted. It brought to my awareness possible old feelings and id's I may have had towards not respecting myself and how this has also carried into my relationships.

A few hours before receiving the e-mail with this writing assignment, I had been contemplating a disagreement I had with my husband. I realized I was carrying my relationship with my father into the marriage - after much focus on NOT doing this. Old patterns were creeping up of staying a safe distance as to not get myself hurt and fearing wrath.

The realization then occurred this was more than my relationship with my paternal father – it was a perceived relationship with "God the Father" coming up. I was projecting my relationship with God into my life and marriage and onto males. My relationship with God growing up was one of deep love, reverence, and fear – the same as I had toward my parental father. We were taught to love AND fear the *Father*.

I was sinking into this awareness when I received the e-mail with this writing assignment. IT was an affirmation to me how I had been raised to love, fear, and revere God and how this great fear of wrath distanced me from males and truly loving relationships with males. I feel this is something that is greatly

I was grateful for this assignment – to go deeper into realizations and to explore any old (unhealthy) feelings I was carrying around into male relationships. I am grateful for the opportunity to love myself more, my husband and my father more and re-pattern my relationship with God the Father. I realized that as I allowed myself to receive the total love from God the Father, I will both receive and have the capacity to give love to males. As I finish these words, my *Daddy* turns 83 in a few hours. I celebrate him with honor and love.

Betsy Hosp
Swami Alishananda
www.powerofonewoman.blogspot.com

COMMENTARY:

It is said that to heal wounds, the hidden must be spoken. In order to have a good relationship as a couple, children need to receive the loving modeling from their parents, other than that, they will find the ways to harmony through struggle, doubt or unintended creations. When a Child that has experienced wounds created by Mother or Father grows as an adult and takes the conscious journey to meet the reasons behind the situation, and openly shares his wounds with the world, he opens up the possibility not only of healing but of transcendence, in this experience then he meets face to face with God, he heals, he forgives and moves forward, gifting his parents with the gift of letting go of entanglements and moving on with his life. Oh such joy for a father and mother is when a child is free and finds his path in life.

My "real" relationship
with the Divine Father energy.
By Swami Deviananda

It is no accident that when I released all my expectations on my birth father, I began to fully acknowledge the loving support of my "real" relationship with the Divine Father energy.

When I was a girl, I was pretty good at feeling sorry for myself. I knew beyond a doubt that my father loved me, yet I couldn't figure out why he "abandoned" me nor why he showed more attention to my "step" brother and sisters over me, and more importantly, why he didn't understand who I was.

When I was nine, I decided to run away. I had $5 dollars in my pocket and since we were camping, I thought it would be easy to catch a ride to California and live with my mom. When I got to the store, a picture of Jesus spoke to me, and we made an agreement. I agreed to stay and find out what love means, and he would protect me further on this journey. At this point, even though I didn't know it "consciously" as a girl, I could feel an unseen hand guiding me as I grew up. Though I still continued to feel lost into my adulthood, I always felt guided and possessed a strong intuitive sense that I trusted deeply. Until this moment, I had no memory of this agreement. During this life journey, I have actively worked in changing many perceptions around God, men and my father because I stayed and kept my agreement as Jesus kept his.

Now I've come to a place where I feel absolutely connected to the Divine Father – the masculine energy that creates movement, provides support and goes beyond any human concept I could possible form. Instead I feel in great harmony with this energy, for engaging with it has giving me discernment and knowing what's mine and what's not, and safe comprehension in journeying between outer and inner worlds. When

I'm centered, I feel a firm love within me. The Divine Feminine gives the material and my gratitude provides access to abundance, while the Divine Masculine provides awareness, a sense of safety and a knowing of all that there is. This knowing comes to me through words and an active mind. Though in my mind, I still have a journey with further life explorations, there isn't a doubt that I have a clear connection with an engaged Divine Father.

Martha Kinkade
Aka Swami Deviananda
www.sacredrebirthing.com

COMMENTARY:

Again we see the importance of safety, an essential energy and gift that the Father can give to a child. It is an essential value, and a most needed energy for our planet these days. Children DESERVE to live and feel safe, and the Father, has this power within to provide for this. He may not know it, yet when he remembers, when he awakens, when he sets his priorities in order, his natural powers unfold, his sense as a protector awakens, and as he hears the call to be initiated as a man, he realizes that he has within what his children need: safety, solidity, respect and love… and through giving this selflessly, he becomes The Divine Father.

The Two Essential Elements of Creation

By Fernando

To me, father is one of the two essential elements of creation. Without father and mother there is no creation and therefore father is as much part of the life creation process as mother is. Both are necessary conditions and thus are complementary in this process. Everything in the universe springs from this father/mother creative process, which in essence is a process of balance. This balance becomes what we are truly in origin, and where our wellbeing and happiness resides. From this perspective, father is part of the equation, as it requires the feminine to truly give birth. This we can see in every aspect of the planet, and the universe, as the feminine energy feeds of the masculine and they jointly integrate vitality and the life force. To me, this father energy potentially represents the strength of the warrior, the benevolence of the king, the wisdom of the magician and the heart of the lover, all in their supreme masculine potentialities. I see father in everything that exists, as everything comes from there and has father energy in it, be it a man, or a woman, or a plant (the corn, for example, has been identified for centuries with this energy) in my family of origin, my father was always present in his way, with his beliefs, but always present. This was very positive as a soother for the strength in my mother's character, and in a way they both carried both the feminine and the masculine energies, both half the father and the mother within them, as we all do.

Warm regards,
Fernando M.

COMMENTARY:

The universe cerates itself from both feminine and masculine energies, it births and rebirths consistently, a sacred dance of polarities, a blissful embrace of diversity. A union of cosmic power consistently happening through the intelligent space. This movement, this dance, resides within each of our souls, and within this movement we find thousands of universes being created, being expanded and collapsed just for the joy of creation. Such is the importance of the Father energy.

The Energy of Responsibility
By Jim Walsh

Father energy to me is the energy of responsibility, of strong foundations, and stability. It is the house over our heads and the streets that we drive on. It is impersonal but all-inclusive. It is the energy we can draw from to lead us to our human destiny. It is the energy that contains the maturation of the warrior; the wisdom of the teacher; the gravitas of the king and the embrace of the lover. It unites with the feminine to manifest physical form and create order from chaos. It is a pathway in us all.

Jim Walsh
www.mindmatterresearch.org

COMMENTARY:

Within the Father energy the true heroic journey can be found. In it, a woman awakens, a man is initiated, a universe is created, chaos is soothed, and peace is birthed in alignment with the universal laws, where the hero in his journey takes full responsibility of its creation, protects the feminine energy, and moves forward, and fearlessly to create better worlds for the sake of the journey and for the benefit of all sentient beings thus a true warrior then is born. Aho!

Now it is YOUR TURN to
Write a Letter to Your Father.

Letter to my Father

By _____ **(Add your name)**

*It doesn't matter who my father was; it matters
who I remember he was. Anne Swxton*

_____

_____

_____

_____

_____

_____

_____

_____

_____

_____

_____

_____

_____

_____

PART VIII

The Inspirations

"Any man can be a father, but it takes a special person to be a dad"
Proverb

The Inspirations

There were men who held me like I wished my father had,
who let me shed the shame I had carried, wholet me find
a love I had never known— self-love. ~Paul Goldman

This section is meant to inspire, motivate, and serve as a refreshing reminder of the love of the Divine Father for all, and the love of all for the Divine Father. It is also helpful to read and visualize your own father and deepen the love, forgiveness and connection with him.

Read, meditate upon this, and perhaps, you may be inspired to write your own set of inspirations, and finally embrace the divine masculine energy... not as a ruler, or as a tyrant, but as the most benevolent guardian, protector of humankind, and the powerful warrior energy whose true essence and mission is the attainment of Peace.

Protective Force of the Universe

Oh Father,
Oh beloved protective force of humanity,
In thy arms are the traces of the labor of creation
Oh beloved masculine energy,
Sweet man and boy, and energy of leadership
Eternally grateful I am for thy sweet silent steadiness.
Beyond emotions you have come to share the sensibility
of the importance that is thy presence.
May you receive back what you have given.
May all beings recognize the importance of your presence.
And may all beings reside in the safety of your manifestation.

Aho!　`

Tender Warrior

How is it that such fragility hides in tender warriorship?
How can we forfeit war for the manifestation
of peace with thy guidance?
Oh sweet father, all what thou have endured for the
sake of the Mother so she can bear the children in her
arms while the work is taken place in thy steps.
Oh sweet man, I recognize you.
You are not alone.
The divine is within you and supports you
like a mother would his child.
Oh Father, oh young man, oh child…
The elders are here to support you.
I am in awe of your grace and the strength of your survival.
I am in gratitude for your steadiness
And in humble recognition of your beauty.
I pay tribute to thee, oh Tender Warrior!

Aho! ~

Peaceful Heart

Father, forgive your children for not realizing that
your silence is the words of goals in motion.
Forgive our neediness to demand from you
a smile, things and affection.
How blind how we have been for there has been not a moment where
your love hasn't embraced us in the most powerful and sublime ways.
Oh father, without guilt, we raise in thy magnificence,
We honor thy place in time
And we salute the strength of your peaceful heart.

Aho! ~

The Ultimate Teacher

Dearest teacher,
Mentor,
Leader,
Elder of the Tribe,
We salute you,
All the women and the children,
We support you,
All animal kingdom,
We embrace you,
All celestial beings
We adore you.

Aho! ~

Rite of Passage

To the boy that grows in to adult-ship
Take these blessings in thy right of passage,
May all women let go when its time
With serenity, surrender, and the strength of a lioness
May you boy, in thy walk towards the land that
he ancestors have visited before you
Know that the women and the men of the
Earth are here to support thee.
The feminine energy of creation is as powerful as the male is,
Yet we drop as women all competition,
All needs to prove our gifts,
All victimization
As we rise in our own goddess power in response
to your impeccable modeling.
Go boy! ~ Rise!
The women are here~
Awaken boy, laugh!
And walk in safety with the mentors of spirit that will guide you.
You have our blessing
It is time to grow!

Aho! ~

Divine Role Model

"Every father should remember that one day his son will follow his example instead of his advice" Unknown

Fathers of men,
Allow your boys to grow,
Not in your shadow but In your brilliant example of uniqueness
Oh father of both female and male spirits,
Wise in the modeling of grace, reverence,
respect and value oriented living.
Oh fathers of the world, may kindness be within thy every act and
thought so that your children can follow your steps of greatness.
Oh fathers, love the mothers, for thy children can inherit
this gift and pass it to the next generations.
Oh fathers, in thy hearts resides the peace on Earth.
You are the Divine Role Model.

Aho! ~

The Mentor

Brothers of Brothers,
The mentor awakens,
Not in to control and power
But into gentle strength.
Oh brothers of men,
Awaken!
Light up the spirit within those whose steps are of young souls
And that are here to live the legacy of your creation
Oh brothers of spirit,
Rest now,
As in your acts
And through thy will
The children of the mother will rise in ascension and joy.
Oh brothers of Source,
Acknowledge the portal that you are
For the sacred masculine energy
To bless all brothers,
And all souls! ~

Aho! ~

Hu-man

Man;
Kindred spirit
Born from Woman.
Man; elegance in motion you are.
Man: harmony resides in thy thoughts
Man: violence in thy heart is no more.
Man; coming back to what is good and kind.
Man; surrendering to the Earth and its healthy boundaries.
Man; respecting universal laws.
Man; allowing God to love you.

Aho! ~

Spirit of the Universe

Oh male energy
For eons thou have protected and have seen thyself alone
Know that the mother sees you
Know that the Earth recognizes the longing, and
The thirst of companionship and brotherhood in your soul.
Traditions of connection will support thee,
Initiation rites will strengthen thee.
Oh sacred male, sacred MAN
The spirit of the universe sustains you with its heart.

Aho! ~

Love the Boy and the Man Shall Rise

Woman,
Both male and female you are.
Salute thy feminine power and respect masculinity.
Be not a victim, and seek no rescue and the rescue shall take place.
A divine paradox.
Speak up to the male energy,
Be certain and in thy power.
Humanity rises with every part of creation in order.
Your power is of birth and rebirth.
The male exists none without thee, and thee exist none without male.
Female power, rise in me,
Female power surrender to the soul in me.
Both man and woman are male and female,
In this, separation disappears
Unity emerges
WOMAN: Love the boy and the man will rise!
As the Holy Spirit breathes as one.

Aho! ~

Ancestral Grace

Ancestors,
Oh grandfathers,
Clear all that was left incomplete in your
time so your generations to follow
Carry the staff of harmonic coherence.
Oh grandfathers, respect thy woman and thy children
So the next generations can build civilizations of peace.
I thank you in the name of the men.
I thank you in the name of the women.
I thank you in the name of the child.
I thank you in the name of the spirit.
Blessed be oh grandfathers blessed be! ~

Aho!

Time to Rest

*"The most important thing a father can do for his
children is to love their mother." Theodore Hesburgh*

Tears shed in quiet moments,
Silently spread without anyone watching.
Yours was a survival strategy…
Its time to rest
In the arms of the divine feminine
Oh sweet man, sweet beloved, surrender your head in to her heart
You deserve this
You are to know her love for thee.
You have not to compete with her,
As she is on your side.
You have nothing to fear
For she sees the inner fire burning of your desire to merge with her.
Beloved man,
Come to me.

Aho! ~

Ultimate Power

At night you sleep, and you become a child again.
The king, the warrior, the master...all in dreamtime travel the same.
No more struggle,
No more starvation, no more war.
Awaken then in the peace of the unity you bring here.
Take your first step in the morning towards being present.
This is the signature that represents the true man.
Invoke presence,
While awake or asleep,
Invoke love.
This is the ultimate masculine power.

Aho! ~

The Ultimate Archetype

Child bearer,
Your seed contains the DNA of God.
Child bearer, treat conception as the portal
where you also came through.
Child bearer, be gentle in the touch and strong in thy commitments.
Child bearer, AS THE ULTIMATE ARCHETYPE,
you are the father of humanity
And the emissary of leadership in the world.

Child bearer, both the mother and father reside in you,
Aho! ~

Vulnerability

To be free of the past,
Oh man, forgive the men in your lineage that by
ignorance could have inherited pain in thee.
Forgive and be free and end all quarrels through this power.
It is now the time for inner peace to manifest as a reality.
Man: forgive!
Man: with this end all tyrant acts, and rise in the model
of integrity, synergy, reverence and humility.
These are the qualities of a warrior! ~
Nothing can defeat you except your thoughts,
Nothing can hurt you except wrong doings towards others.
Cease all violence now!
Cease all anger now!
Cease all envy now!
I believe you!
I believe in you!
Now live it!
TAKE ACTION, NOW!

Aho!

Free of Entanglements

The son and the father need time alone to
walk in the forest of modeling.
Absolute respect and sacredness must be shared with every step.
The son and the father must walk in mutual understanding.
No one right, no one wrong...everything in divine order.
The father models possibilities, the child manifests opportunities.
The father lives his life and lets his son live his, and then, the moment
comes when the father surrenders his son to the wise ones.
The son loves the father,
The father loves the son
And without entanglements the new civilization rebirths in peace.
As Father and Son are ONE.

Aho! ~

Father Wisdom, Daughter Safety

The daughter and the father,
What sweet encounter. Fathers' gentleness sets the tone for her future.
Oh father, be impeccable in your thoughts as
thy daughters read thy silence well.
Thy touch shall be of respect and recognition that the girl
will become a woman and will find her path of wisdom.
Let her go,
She doesn't belong to you.
Stay in your place of father,
She is a child,
Take care of her as God would.
As you are not his owner but an assistant of the Great Spirit.
Thank you father for recognizing the wisdom in your daughters' heart.
Thank you

Aho! ~

Success

Bless your child oh father when the cord is ready to be cut.
Let him be free and bless your child endlessly in all his chosen steps.
Father, dear male energy,
Bless every step your children choose to take,
and with this bless your own path.
You are the portal of possibilities and manifestation.
Model wisely! ~
Eat healthy! ~
Strive for success in the now!!!

Aho!

Child of God

Father; remember you are a child,
And source will ever provide for you.
As you do your work, oh father!, remember
that you are the beloved of the creator.
You are more than a label of man, father, boy, or masculine energy.
You are the child of God.
Say it loud:
I AM THE CHILD OFGOD
I AM THE MANIFESTATION OF SOURCE
I AM BEYOND LABELS
I AM!

Aho!

The Beloved

We need each other, male and female. We need a balance
of energies, masculine and feminine. ~ Jeanie Marshall

You are the beloved of the sacred feminine,
Without you she feels incomplete.
With you she finds her strength.
In your powerful arms she melts continuously.
Thank you for the safety you offer with your life.
She acknowledges your gift, and walks fearlessly in the planet.
Beloved of creation…the divine feminine surrenders to you.

Aho! ~

The Source

Oh Shiva,
Oh Vishnu,
Oh Brahma,
Oh Krishna,
Oh Jesus,
Oh Moses,
Oh Buddha,
Oh Gandhi,
Oh Babaji,
Oh Holy Chief,
Oh Holy Spirit
Bring the blessings to me,
As I say three times with my hearts' pled:
Aho! Aho! Aho!
Aham Brahmas mi![48]

---

48 "I", *Brahma* means Brahman the creator, God or the *Parabrahman*, the supreme
spirit and *Asmi* means am. So put together, *Aham Brahmasmi* means "I am Brahma,"
or rather I am the creator or I am god.

PART IX

Tribute Quotes
21 Days of Tribute
Offered to the Fathers of Humanity

*Blessed indeed is the man who hears many gentle voices call
him father! ~Lydia M. Child, Philothea: A Romance, 1836*

Tribute Quotes

The next section is a compilation of inspirational quotes by some of the greatest minds in our planet. They are offered as a tribute to all the male/father energy that exists and has ever existed. It is suggested that you choose one or two quotes and share it with those who you think carry these attributes. Paying tribute is one of the greatest gifts we can give to one another..

If you choose, you can use a quote a day for 21 days to pay tribute every day to a man you honor, with this you will not only create the habit of paying tribute, but also to raise the frequency of honoring your own male energies.

Tribute Quotes, 21 Days of Tribute

1. One father is more than a hundred Schoolemasters. ~George Herbert, Outlandish Proverbs, 1640
2. Sometimes the poorest man leaves his children the richest inheritance. ~Ruth E. Renkel
3. The father who would taste the essence of his fatherhood must turn back from the plane of his experience, take with him the fruits of his journey and begin again beside his child, marching step by step over the same old road. ~Angelo Patri
4. My father, when he went, made my childhood a gift of a half a century. ~Antonio Porchia, Voces, 1943, translated from Spanish by W.S. Merwin
5. It is much easier to become a father than to be one. ~Kent Nerburn, Letters to My Son: Reflections on Becoming a Man, 1994
6. The words that a father speaks to his children in the privacy of home are not heard by the world, but, as in whispering-galleries, they are clearly heard at the end and by posterity. ~Jean Paul Richter
7. Any man can be a father. It takes someone special to be a dad. ~Author Unknown
8. The greatest gift I ever had Came from God; I call him Dad! ~Author Unknown
9. I love my father as the stars - he's a bright shining example and a happy twinkling in my heart. ~Adabella Radici
10. Two little girls, on their way home from Sunday school, were solemnly discussing the lesson. "Do you believe there is a devil?" asked one. "No," said the other promptly. "It's like Santa Claus: it's your father." ~Ladies' Home Journal, quoted in 2,715 One-Line Quotations for Speakers, Writers & Raconteurs by Edward F. Murphy

11. Dad, your guiding hand on my shoulder will remain with me forever. ~Author Unknown

12. Sherman made the terrible discovery that men make about their fathers sooner or later... that the man before him was not an aging father but a boy, a boy much like himself, a boy who grew up and had a child of his own and, as best he could, out of a sense of duty and, perhaps love, adopted a role called Being a Father so that his child would have something mythical and infinitely important: a Protector, who would keep a lid on all the chaotic and catastrophic possibilities of life. ~Tom Wolfe, The Bonfire of the Vanities

13. Old as she was, she still missed her daddy sometimes. ~Gloria Naylor

14. You will find that if you really try to be a father, your child will meet you halfway. ~Robert Brault

15. Sons are for fathers the twice-told tale. ~Victoria Secunda, Women and Their Fathers, 1992

16. Why are men reluctant to become fathers? They aren't through being children. ~Cindy Garner

17. Fathers represent another way of looking at life - the possibility of an alternative dialogue. ~Louise J. Kaplan, Oneness and Separateness: From Infant to Individual, 1978

18. There's something like a line of gold thread running through a man's words when he talks to his daughter, and gradually over the years it gets to be long enough for you to pick up in your hands and weave into a cloth that feels like love itself. ~John Gregory Brown, Decorations in a Ruined Cemetery, 1994

19. There are three stages of a man's life: He believes in Santa Claus, he doesn't believe in Santa Claus, he is Santa Claus. ~Author Unknown

20. Fatherhood is pretending the present you love most is soap-on-a-rope. ~Bill Cosby

21. When I was a boy of fourteen, my father was so ignorant I could hardly stand to have the old man around. But when I got to be twenty-one, I was astonished at how much he had learned in seven years. ~Mark Twain, "Old Times on the Mississippi" Atlantic Monthly, 1874

PART X

Epilogue
Until the Next Time

In the faces of men and women I see God.
Walt Whitman

For dear ones,
This is your life,
This is the time where we can get together and heal the planet.
There is no more time to waste.
Let us serve the mother, let us support the father,
Let us embrace the love as couples,
Let us model to the children this love.
Let us be kind to our sons and listen to them,
And let us be kind to our daughters and respect their wisdom.
Let us come back to restoration and common sense love.
Let us come back to love.
Time is of the essence; Time is at hand

Babaji Nagaraj

Phuro! Be Inspired

This book awakens such love and gratitude for my father. I always felt safe and supported by him. He was a very simple man, a factory worker and a lover of nature. He never went beyond the 6th grade, and yet I could always turn to him for advice and inspiration. When he had no answer, no advice, he gave me the gift of silence and space, or the gift of humor. He had the wisdom to let life be my teacher; to let me find my own answer.

My father gave me unconditional love. He taught me so many practical and profound things: from how to ride a bike and drive a car, to how to shoot a gun and a bow; from how to fish and swim, to how to sing and sharpen a knife. He taught me to cherish myself, and my loved ones. He taught me tolerance and patience, He how to squeeze all the juice out every precious moment in life. And he inspired me to worship the Divine Mother.

One of the greatest gifts my father gave me was the gift of freedom. The freedom to be, to learn and grow in my own way and in my own time: he taught me to follow my own path no matter where it led or what others said. Somehow he was willing to trust something in me more than he did his own ideas about how I should be.

With his gifts of freedom and safety and love, I found my own power, I found my own voice, and I found my own way. I went beyond anyone in my family, and I learned things that my father could never know. And he was wise enough and humble enough in those moments to let me be his teacher. And in doing that, he was teaching me to trust the Divine Father in me!

This book gives us an opportunity to learn from many great teachers.

And it gives us the space to learn from the great teacher within.

Open this book anywhere and you will receive a gift.
Turn to any page, and you will harvest a pearl.
Live this book and you will find wisdom.
It's a book my father would love.
Phuro! ("Be inspired!")

Dan Brule
President
Breath Mastery
www.breathmastery.com

About the Author

Ivonne Delaflor (Aka) **Swami Amenai** is the *Founder and President of Delaflor Teachings International,* founder of Mastery Life A.C. and co-founder of the Higher School for Conscious Evolution. She is the author of The Positive Child through the Language of Love, Mastering Life, Sacred Messages for the Parents of the World, Divine Mother, India; The Journey of a Lifetime, The Book of Origins, Stop Wasting Your Time & Start Doing what Matters Most, and  Invitation to love. Has published several articles for Tibetan women magazines, Integral life and several Ezine articles on leadership, synergy and the importance of self-actualization.

She is a certified Total Awareness Coach and certified Parent Talk trainer and has studied Sacred Shamanic Rebirth, Body Language, Constellation Therapy, Breath Therapy, and is a Reiki Master. She has done more than 500 hours of personal work at BEBA, a non-profit organization that supports healthy bonding and attachment for infants and their parents and is a graduate of The School for The Work with Byron Katie, and the Futuring School with Stefan Hermann. She is also a graduate of the Platinum Mentoring Coaching with Brian Tracy and has a career in Fitness and Nutrition, She is a Certified RAW Nutritionist from the School of David Wolfe, and has a Masters in Business Administration.

Ivonne has been initiated into Babaji's ancient Kriya Yoga tradition and received initiations (shaktipat) directly from Babaji...whom she met one on one in Rishikesh India in the year 2003. She was also initiated as Swami Amenanda, lovingly called by students and friends Amenai, receiving her name by direct request of Babaji Nagaraj. She is an initiate of the Maitri Violet-Silver Chord Order - http://www.maitriorder.com.

Ivonne has a gift to support others to find their life mission and set it in motion. She also does private sessions and Ascended Master Spiritual Readings per request.

She is the creator of The Codes of AH & the Founder of the Transcendental Rebirthing System created since 2006, supporting ecstatic rebirth of the whole being into brilliancy and repatterning awareness. Ivonne currently shares her time Cancun with her three children and her beloved and life partner, Toby Alexander.

Her new books; Unplug!, The Spiritual Face of Autism, The Rebirth of Humanity, The RAWsurrection, & Making Amends Now will be published in 2013.

For scheduling Private Mentoring Sessions, or Ascended Master Spiritual readings, you may contact Ivonne via email at: hsfce@higherschoolforconsciousevolution.com, or at amenai@higherschoolforconsciousevolution.com

Other Books by the Author

You can find the books of Ivonne Delaflor at all online book retailers or by emailing us at hsfce@higherschoolforconsciousevolution.com

India: The Journey of a Lifetime - Paperback (Mar. 7, 2005) by Ivonne Delaflor

Your Soulmate Called God - Paperback (Mar. 16, 2005) by Ivonne Delaflor

Invitation To Love: 108 Reminders for the Enlightened Ones - Paperback (Jan. 26, 2005) by Ivonne Delaflor

The Positive Child: Through the Language of Love - Paperback (Sept. 23, 2004) by Ivonne Delaflor

Mastering Life: Co-creating a Reality of Love Through the Power of Sharing - Paperback (Jan. 5, 2005) by Ivonne Delaflor

Divine Mother: Devotional Offerings for the Sacred Feminine within All Beings - Paperback (July 19, 2007) by Ivonne Delaflor

Sacred Messages: for the Parents of the World - Paperback (Feb. 19, 2006) by Ivonne Delaflor and Phil LaHaye

Stop Wasting Your Time and Start Doing What Matters Most: A Wake-Up Call for True Leadership [Paperback], Jeffrey Krug (Author), Ivonne Delaflor Alexander (Author)

Unplug! The Ascended Masters Speak, Ivonne Delaflor Alexander and Sylvia Dokter

The RAWsurrection; Living RAW beyond Food, Ivonne Delaflor Alexander and Gustavo Castaner

SUGGESTED LINKS

www.ivonnedelaflor.com
www.higherschoolforconsciousevolution.com
www.transcendentalrebirthing.com
www.dnaperfection.com

MEDIA

FOLLOW US ON TWITTER: https://twitter.com/#!/Amenai
FOLLOW US ON FACEBOOK: https://www.facebook.com/HSFCE
SUBSCRIBE TO MY FREE BLOG: http://rawnestliving.wordpress.com/
WATCH US ON YOU TUBE: http://youtu.be/GXcuSoz0HFY

SPEAKING ENGAGEMENTS

To Request for Private Workshops, School Presentations, Leadership Trainings, or Speaking Engagements with Ivonne Delaflor please contact:

Swami Bharatananda at: bharata@transcendentalrebirthing.com

Or hsfce@higherschoolforconsciousevolution.com